TAKING OFF

For Richard, Nicholas and James
In memory of Marianne

TAKING OFF

The Story of the Mull Little Theatre

BARRIE HESKETH

THE NEW IONA PRESS

Acknowledgements

I wish to thank the Michael Marks Charitable Trust and Churchill College, Cambridge for enabling me to take time out to write the first draft of this book.

My thanks also go to the many Friends of the Mull Little Theatre, too many to mention by name, who forwarded me copies of the Mull Little Theatre newsletters, Marianne's correspondence, programmes, photographs and other invaluable background material.

Special thanks go to my partner in everything, Philippa Comber, without whose unflagging encouragement and support over the past ten years as well as her sensitive literary advice, this book would have remained 'a thing of shreds and patches'.

BH

All photographs and illustrations loaned by the author. For kind permission to reproduce the following, the publisher wishes to thank: Cordelia Oliver (photo by the late George A. Oliver, p.76); Scottish Field (photos by Geo. B. Alden, pp 24, 25, 51).

Front cover: Marianne and Barrie Hesketh at the Mull Little Theatre, *c.* 1980–83. Every effort has been made to trace the photographer, without success. Any information will be welcomed by the publisher.
Frontispiece and back cover: linocut of Mull Little Theatre by Barrie Hesketh.

The publisher gratefully acknowledges subsidy from the Scottish Arts Council towards the production of this book.

THE SCOTTISH **ARTS** COUNCIL

© Barrie Hesketh 1997

ISBN 0-9516283-8-0
A catalogue record for this book is available from the British Library.

Typeset by Posthouse Printing & Publishing, Findhorn
Printed in Great Britain by Redwood Books, Trowbridge
for
The New Iona Press
7 Drynie Terrace, Inverness IV2 4UP

Contents

Foreword

Magic Mull. It is not surprising that Barrie and Marianne chose to present *The Tempest* during the first years of their brilliant brainchild, the Mull Little Theatre.

This island is a place of inspiration, and the ingenuity and devotion with which the Heskeths pursued their dream of giving the islanders and their visitors a diet of good writing, good theatre – often outstandingly so – together with wonderfully imaginative visual effects, was moving and stirring proof not only of the success of their enterprise but also of the life-giving spirit of the island itself.

They raised their three sons there, and they did what they wanted and needed to do – to act, direct, paint. All the talents demanded by the theatre they provided with joy and flair. They were fortunate people, and they worked very hard indeed to deserve their fortune.

Their theatre was a barn, beautifully transformed into a perfect little theatre, pretty and comfortable, with cushions everywhere, good coffee and delicious homemade cakes for the intervals. They did everything themselves.

This is a story of creative fulfilment ending in deep sadness, a story of artistry and perseverance and love.

There must be many who count themselves lucky to have been there and seen for themselves. As I do.

Paul Scofield

1

First Call

Stories. When I was very little, my father told me stories; he made them up. Later, he would read them to me. My mother also told me stories – but rarely read them. From my earliest days, she introduced me to the classic fairy tales and the great stories of Greece and Rome, preferring to add ornaments of her own devising. She told me the sagas of the Nordic countries and magical tales from Persia and India. Most of all, she relied on Ancient Greek mythology. I took everything in, more than half believingly. Time would show how greatly this experience was to influence my work in the theatre.

I was born in Erdington in Birmingham on 11 April 1930. It was a part of town for the middle classes, where there were fields and parks and streets lined with trees. Our road was very wide, and outside my parents' house was a procession of fine beeches. In autumn the leaves would rise in tides over my red wellingtons.

When I was six, I was permitted to find my own way to my father's parents who lived close by. I spent a lot of time with my granny, Olivia, but avoided my grandfather. I remember him as a grumpy old man who rode a bicycle round the local streets with his hands off the handlebars. Before he retired to Birmingham he had been a strict headmaster at Selby Grammar School.

Granny Olivia was slim and petite. She wore a black choker and there was an intriguing hardness about her hugs. She explained that something had gone wrong with one of her breasts and she'd had to have it cut off. I accepted this as part of life and so did she.

Granny was a passionate Methodist and deeply committed to 'doing good' in the area. So much good, in fact, that a local road was named after her: Hesketh Crescent. This proved to have small but far-reaching results for me thirty years on. But more of that later.

My parents stayed in Erdington until before the Second World War. Then, with gas-masks being handed out in little, square cardboard boxes and the Munich Crisis worrying everyone except the most gullible, we decided to get out of the city before it was bombed. My mother and father had no illusions about the horrors of war . They chose to return to my mother's home in Buxton – the Victorian spa town that nestles high up in the Peak District. They thought – rightly as it turned out – that there we would be safer from the bombing if and when it happened.

With financial assistance from various members of the family, my father bought a village shop on the Derbyshire/Staffordshire border. The official name for that particular collection of farms and barns was Quarnford, but the place was known locally as Flash, a name it had earned in a previous century when the village had been a centre for the production of counterfeit money.

The shop itself, situated in the middle of the bleakest of moorscapes, reminded me of the village stores in Chaplin's film *The Gold Rush*. It was a wooden structure, with shutters that could be clamped tight with iron bars. From out of its corrugated iron roof stuck an iron chimney. The stove inside exactly matched the ones in the film sets. In winter, it was so stoked up with coke that it glowed red all over, appearing to have a life of its own as dark bands of blue and black meandered over the heated surface.

Winters were terrible. Sometimes the snow drifts would cover the road up to twenty feet high and my father would be snowbound for days. To my young eyes, it seemed that everything in the world was on display and for sale. The materials for making up clogs and boots hung on nails driven into the walls. Glass-fronted cupboards were stocked with bales of cloth for farmers' wives to sew into garments for themselves and their families. Workers' dungarees lay stiff and lifeless in dark corners. Tins, boxes and sacks were everywhere. Hanging from the rafters amongst the cured hams, swung the pots and pans, saws, brushes, bicycle tyres and storm lanterns. There were scythes and farm implements; sledgehammers and handyman's tools leant against the counters. Big, round cheeses like millstones – far too heavy for me to carry – lay on a marble slab. Dark treacle oozed from a black and gold canister abutting the bacon machine: 'Get your hands away from that, Barrie!' Behind a wooden screen festooned with posters advertising Craven 'A' cigarettes, Ovaltine, Virol and Sunlight soap, there were large bins filled with corn, oatmeal, flour and fragrant cattle-cake. Outside in front stood an ancient petrol pump that had to be wound up by hand before it would deliver fuel. Next to this ratchet-and-cog machine was an evil-smelling shack that housed large tanks containing paraffin and motor oil. A chemical lavatory – a galvanised bucket with a can of disinfectant standing beside it – lurked behind a creaking door.

There were times during school holidays when I went up to the shop to help. One of the clearest memories I have is of the bank of little black drawers behind the counter. In these was kept a huge variety of bric-à brac needed by the farming community – tobacco twist, matches, pipe-cleaners, lighter flints. The only other time I ever saw drawers like these was when I moved to Mull. A farmer, having bought his ounce of twist, would stand by the stove. He'd take out a large pen-knife, open it and wipe the blade on his corduroy trousers. The twist, which was dark brown, oily, and sold in portions about the size of a bicycle brake-block, was held with a broad thumb supporting one side to counter the pressure from the cut of the knife. The farmer's thumb-nail, blackened, long, serrated at the edge and sticking up beyond the stub of twist, seemed to be an essential adjunct to the process of preparing a 'chew'. After cutting the slice and transferring it to the mouth on the knife blade, there was a moment of comparative quiet while the saliva was worked up. Then, suddenly, a stream of dark brown juice would shoot from between blackened teeth and jet unerringly on to the small patch of red hot coals just visible through a hole in the top of the stove. There, for a brief second, it would sizzle fiercely.

My father had made a great effort to integrate himself into the community. However, one winter something happened that, in the main, turned him against it. A man fell from a tractor close to his shop, not twenty yards from the local inn. He was trapped beneath the machine. My father appealed to the people enjoying a drink in the bar to come out and help him release the poor man. According to my father, not one of them responded. He returned to the victim and, to give what comfort and warmth he could, he first wrapped him in sacking brought from the shop. Then, for the rest of the night, he lay down beside him in the snow. It was to no avail; the man did not survive.

Eventually, I wrote up this incident as a television play. For the purposes of drama, I developed the story as it stood and invented characters to bring out my theme of death by default. I offered it to a director at the Granada Television studios in Manchester (situated only thirty miles from where the tragedy had occurred) but he handed it back to me with the comment that no such thing could happen in modern-day Britain. That play, *The Cold Heart*, was later broadcast on the radio with Wilfred Pickles in the lead.

Moving from the city to a country town widened my horizons. I was a healthy lad, living mostly outdoors in the fields and woods. The war more or less passed us by. After hostilities had ceased, some property which had been in the family's possession and was about to be sold, became vacant. In the early part of the century, this property had been their town house and a chemist's shop combined; during the war it had been rented to a Jewish family, refugees from Nazi Germany. Before the old shop was sold, I went with my mother and her sister, Gertrude, to view it. I was transported into another world. The shop part remained very much as it always had been. The tenants had had no use for it and had kept it locked up. I was able to see where my grandfather, Isaac, and his son, Raymond, had kept their pots – blue for poisons, pink for unguents, white for powders. I was shown the ring-stains on dusty shelves left by the tightly-stoppered glass jars of narcotics, including one that had contained a large ball of laudanum – a powerful painkiller, regularly prescribed for toothache, migraine and fractious babies. Pill boxes lay on the working surfaces together with other containers that had held seaweed and leeches. The shell of a tortoise was suspended over the dusty fireplace.

I do not remember for sure, but since my Aunt Gertrude was an inveterate quoter, I hazard a guess that she would have declaimed Shakespeare's description of the apothecary's shop from *Romeo and Juliet*: 'And in his shop a tortoise hung, an alligator stuffed, and on his shelves, a beggarly account of empty boxes, green earthen pots, bladders, and musty seeds'. Both sides of the family had always prided themselves in knowing the classics – and imparting them.

2

Beginners Please

At the age of twenty-one, I left home in Buxton to enrol as a student at Central School of Speech and Drama in London. This is now housed at the Embassy Theatre in Swiss Cottage; but when I was a student in 1951 it was within the Royal Albert Hall. The offices and practice rooms followed the curve of the outside wall of the big circular building and were to be found towards the back, overlooking the Royal College of Music and the highly ornate College of Organists. The Central School theatre also followed the curve. The auditorium was wide and narrow, with seating which could be cleared away so that students could use the floor as a practice area.

The first class I attended was led by Stephen Joseph, who later introduced theatre-in-the-round to Britain. He invited us to improvise a dockyard scene. We began disporting ourselves as drunks, pimps, whores, spivs and sailors. This was the first improvisation I'd ever done and I felt diffident. I thought that if I pretended to be very drunk, any mistake I might make would be seen as the effect of assumed inebriation.

I set off across the room. Standing in my way was a girl with the most marvellous brown eyes. She wore a red tartan skirt and a green jersey that swelled over her large bust. She stood firmly and had the strong legs of a dancer. Because my character was proving more difficult than expected – it wasn't easy to be convincingly drunk when I was not – I was looking for any excuse to hide my inadequacy. I threw my arms round the girl's neck and stuttered, 'Kish me!'

These were the first words I ever spoke to Marianne. She told me afterwards she had hated me immediately. She didn't know what to do and thought I'd done it deliberately to make a fool of her. We just clung to each other – she looking daggers at me, while I kept repeating 'Kish me!' With slight variations, I kept up the refrain for the next thirty-three years.

Her irritation soon gave way and we found ourselves in each other's company quite often, as though by accident. It was becoming obvious to us, and then to everyone else, that we were a couple. We sought each other out. Our delight in each other first came with friendship: a mutual fondness for all the arts; a shared fascination for French cinema and European culture rather than British theatre; and a cat-like curiosity about everything under the sun. During our second year at Central we took the London University Diploma of Dramatic Art and, as we were so near Exhibition Road, we would often go into the museums to check up on the history of technology, furniture and costume. We became known to our friends as Victoria and Albert.

Marianne's mother, Rita (née Turner), had been born late into an Exeter family and had not been made welcome. Rita's mother – that is, Marianne's grandmother – had been a suffragette and a Fabian. She played the organ in Exeter Cathedral, read Ibsen and drank gin. Indeed, she was often the worse for alcohol and on several occasions Rita had been forced to pour bottles of the stuff down the sink to stop her mother getting at them. On one day each week there would be an 'At Home' when the parents invited their friends round to drink punch. After hearing Mr Turner read the latest edition of the Charles Dickens story, hot off the press, they would take out their stringed instruments and play classical music together. When Rita was old enough to join in the music-making, she sang to their accompaniment. I first got to know her as a lady in her sixties, but the quality of her voice was that of a much younger woman; a light contralto of great power and range. She was always in demand as a singer, but when she was offered a position with the Ben Greet Stage Company – a well-known touring group that was to form the basis of the Old Vic Company in London – she turned the offer down.

Marianne and I had something in common in our recent ancestry, since Rita's father had also been a chemist. Mr Turner had owned a shop in the centre of Exeter behind which there was a research laboratory where he worked assiduously at classifying local poisonous plants. To fund his work, he accepted money from many of the local landowners and, in return, acted as a doctor-cum-chemist to any sick labourer they might send him, treating them for free.

It was customary for chemists to employ a man to fetch and carry. Mr Turner's porter, Mr Richards, was a man of no great intellect but of such a sweet disposition that everyone admired him and bore him affection. He opened and shut the door for customers and helped them in and out of their carriages. Most of his time, however, was spent in delivering bottles of medicine and boxes of pills to needy patients. Each item was beautifully wrapped and tabbed with a little red blob of sealing wax. Mr Richard's youngest son, Percy, was apprenticed to an Exeter bookbinder. One day, on hearing the stirring sound of military drums and bugles, he downed his tools, ran up to the market-place, saluted the recruiting sergeant and took the Queen's shilling, thereby signing on as a regular soldier with the 11th Hussars – the Cherrypickers. He soon discovered himself to be blessed as a natural horseman and was the regimental hunt servant on its tour of Ireland before the regiment embarked for France to fight as part of the army of 'Old Contemptibles' in the First World War. Before leaving

Marianne with Max, the lion cub, photographed at London Zoo by her father, Percy Richards, 1937

for the front, he proposed to Rita and was accepted.

As soon as hostilities ceased, Percy was sent to Kurdistan (then under the British Mandate) to act as an aide to a roving magistrate. The few remaining letters still in the family's possession show him to have been a man of charm and courage.

Later, Marianne was to draw great strength from the fact of having been a soldier's daughter. However, by the time she was born – in 1930 – her father had retired from the army and taken a job as a warder in Wandsworth Prison. This meant that she was brought up within the institution.

Like her parents, she came to dread the days when a man was to be hanged. The eight o'clock chime was not heard on those mornings. Her earliest memories were of lying in a pram while the parole prisoners – those allowed to work around the prison officers' quarters – leant over and talked to her. The men missed the sight of children and obviously took delight in visiting her. Marianne used to speak about one who had startling blue eyes; they used to call him 'Sailor'. He and 'Diamonds' were two prisoners with 'nice faces' who were kind to her.

It took me many years to understand the impact upon Marianne of this early contact with the criminal fraternity. If anything ever got lost or misplaced at home, she automatically concluded that someone had come into the house and stolen it. This would upset me very much. Marianne would wail, 'We'll never see it again,' to which I would retort, rather patronisingly, 'Good God, girl, who'd want to come to Mull and break into our house only to steal the lemon squeezer!' It was some time before it dawned on me that she was not trying to blame a thief – because of course there never was one. Rather it was that, in her most formative years, thieving and other forms of delinquency had been a fact of life.

I found in Marianne a companion who was passionate about everything she did, not least in her desire to get to know London. She loved its history and pageantry. At weekends, we'd pack sandwiches and a thermos flask of tea to visit an art gallery or a National Trust property – Ham House, Kenwood, Box Hill. Because we were on a tight budget, it was the nearby historic buildings, museums and galleries to which we would return again and again, especially the Tate.

Dramatic writing in Britain in the early fifties was a dreadfully dull kind of creature. There was a dreary hangover of plays and imitations of plays that could have been seen in any repertory theatre before the war. One man, Christopher Fry, threw in a handful of fire-crackers with plays like *A Phoenix Too Frequent* and *The Lady's Not for Burning*, but, like fire-crackers, they burst upon an astonished public and then faded out as quickly.

Marianne and I certainly went to the theatre; but we took greatest pleasure in the other arts, particularly the cinema. European films made a big impression upon us. These were mostly to be seen either at the Curzon in Mayfair, which we could only afford about once a term, or at the little cinema half-way down the King's Road in Chelsea – the Classic – which was well within our means. In those days it was possible to sit through a programme several times. As a source of learning, the cinema of the time was, for us, as important as Central itself. The effect of those films, especially the

French and Italian ones, lasted our lifetime together. They were often made on a shoe-string, and we looked to them for inspiration. Later, when we were developing our work on the Isle of Mull, we would refer both consciously and, no doubt, unconsciously to the European culture we had absorbed in London. If we had a personal style, we owed much of it to the experience of holding hands in the Chelsea Classic in the early fifties. Our falling in love coincided with the time we spent absorbing the immaculate techniques of Arletty, Barrault and Jouvet.

Before coming to Central, Marianne had worked at the LEA offices in Wandsworth. In the evenings and at weekends, she attended drama classes at Morley College. Rupert Doon was the drama director, and this extraordinary man of the theatre and ballet world had a lasting influence on her. She danced everywhere. She never stopped. Even thirty years later, in painfully different circumstances, she continued to take pride in the way she carried herself. 'Look', she would say and, extending her arms through a classic gesture, she would smile and add, 'I still have my *port de bras*'.

We took our first holiday together in Felixstowe. It was a working holiday at a children's camp, at which we looked after theatre activities, organised shows and ran improvised theatre games. Marianne and I found ourselves housed together and sharing a bedroom. We simply lay beside each other and talked and talked. We talked about what it would be like to run a theatre of our own. During an afternoon off from caring for the children, we found a local building for sale. We got the keys and, for the first time, we looked at a hall with a serious view to turning it into a theatre. Sensible enough to realise that we did not yet have the expertise to take on such a venture, but not wanting to admit this to each other, we rationalised our decision by taking fierce objection to four boxes of very ancient and putrid Camembert cheese we found mouldering on a shelf. We told ourselves we couldn't possibly run a theatre which had such revolting things in its cupboards – it would pervade the atmosphere for weeks!

It was on 5 December 1953, nearly two years after we had met, that Marianne and I made love for the first time. We had lead parts in the School's Christmas production of Christopher Fry's *The Lady's Not for Burning* and the afternoon before the evening performance had been free. She came round to my room and, at long last, our bodies caught up with our feelings.

The day of the final showcase came and went. It was a stressful but exciting afternoon late in the summer term when, as always, Central had taken over a West End theatre so that the final-year students could each be given a short part to play in front of an invited audience of producers, directors and agents.

After our finals, Marianne and I were both offered jobs out of the country, but we stayed put to be near each other. I turned down an opportunity to tour Germany in *Seagulls Over Sorrento* in favour of a season at Preston Repertory. Marianne refused work with Jersey Repertory Theatre and joined Caryl Jenner Touring Productions. Caryl ran a summer season of repertory at the seaside resorts of Seaford and Southwold. She also sent out tours of plays for both adults and children. I joined the Caryl Jenner Company once my contract with Preston Repertory Theatre had ended.

Marianne's first publicity photo, taken early 1950's

Caryl Jenner was a phenomenon – a legend in theatrical circles. I recollect her as a thin, weedy creature with lank hair, bad teeth, nicotine-stained fingers and a voice pitched deeper than many a man's. My own experience of her was that she liked men and loved women. Caryl was a stern director who did not suffer fools gladly.

Stern though she may have been, she always saw to it that adequate arrangements were made for the comfort of the members of a touring company before we set out. We were once put up by a local worthy in a large rambling house, Ormsby Hall, Cleveland (now a National Trust property). This was in the days when it was not done to say too much about the nature of your relationship with your girlfriend. We decided that I would wait until the house was quiet and then make my way to Marianne's room. I knew exactly where it was in the daytime, but by moonlight everything looked different: the house took on another layout and landmarks were not where I expected them to be. For a while, I was completely lost. I couldn't find any light switches, so I bumped into things – loudly. Then, when I did reach her corridor, I couldn't find her door. I knew I must be in the right place, as I'd previously taken note of a particular picture. I ran my hand along the wall. No door.

I was on the point of going back to my own room when I remembered that some of the doors were set completely flush with the wall. Its position was given away only by the door handle but, since this was recessed into the wooden panel, it was difficult to find. There was more feverish scratching as I groped my way along. Just as I was hoping nobody would find me in this ridiculous and compromising situation, a door opened and Marianne popped her head out and beckoned me in. She'd heard my progress for some time. We concluded that the whole house must have known what I was up to. They also knew when I returned to my own room just before daybreak. The moon had gone behind the clouds and it was pitch black. I knocked into a table with a brass vase on it.

Marianne and I were married on 27 August 1954 in Seaford where we were playing in Caryl's summer repertory company. On the day of the wedding, we took the train to Lewes after the morning's rehearsal. Marianne wore a simple blue dress that was too tight for her across the bust, and a hat borrowed from the theatre wardrobe. Because we had bought her a new handbag, there was no money to spare for flowers. We took a bunch of dried ones from the set of that week's romantic comedy, *Lace On Her Petticoat* by Aimé Stuart, and left, with instructions from Caryl that we were to bring them back – or else!

When the end of the season arrived, we thought about looking for a home – a base from which we could find employment in London. Then, one brisk day, with a few hours to spare, and having taken a bus to Shoreham to look round the harbour, we caught sight of *Rona*. A sign tied to her mast read, 'Boat for Sale'.

Neither of us knew anything about sailing, although we had been attracted by the notion of having a little houseboat on the Thames as our first home. *Rona* was a converted lifeboat, with a cabin and minuscule galley. She was fitted with a sail, as well as a powerful converted Ford T petrol engine built into the section just behind the helmsman's shelter – a cosy, shack-like construction, known as the dog-house.

Barrie, 1955

A sudden windfall, a wedding gift from my mother, made the purchase possible. It didn't take us long to make up our minds – a quick look round the hull of the boat where it rested on the stocks – and yes, to hell with it, why not? And so we became the owners of a boat. The books we then bought – *How to Navigate*, *What to Do in a Storm* and *Cooking on Gimbals* – did nothing to dampen our naive enthusiasm. Nor did the first three weeks on land, making *Rona* seaworthy. We scraped down the hull and repainted it with anti-fouler, a concoction containing arsenic which brought on an uncomfortable rash.

One afternoon, we were invited for a cup of tea on board a neighbouring yacht. Our hostess offered to read my tea leaves. I swirled the cup round, turning it upside down in the saucer to allow the drops of remaining liquid to drain away, and handed it to her. She studied the pattern that the tea leaves had taken on and said she could see an eagle, which she assured me would appear when I was about to become successful. This was the only time I ever had my fortune read.

On a rainy day in late summer, we dragged *Rona* to the water's edge and pushed her in. Our first night afloat was horrible. We had not been prepared for the noise of the waves slapping loudly and continuously against the wooden hull six inches from our ears. Neither were we thrilled at the rain of condensation that dripped on us from our cabin roof. Nor were our tempers improved when a little kitten, a half-Siamese that we'd picked up from a local farm as the ship's mascot, was sick on a pillow. After a fitful night, we struggled on deck at first light to find that a fresh wind had whipped up the waves at the harbour bar; they looked very rough.

A local yachtsman had agreed to be our skipper for the voyage to London. He arrived early and we checked the boat together to make sure that everything was shipshape and Bristol fashion. We started the Ford T engine and, with its dull roar ringing in our ears, set off. We managed the first hundred yards without mishap, then felt the waves resisting us as we approached the harbour bar. Suddenly, the wind gusted, the boat began to corkscrew and we found ourselves being pushed towards the steep, glistening breakwater. The skipper adjusted our course and we made a few more yards; then the engine faltered. Immediately, we felt the wind take advantage of us and begin blowing the boat back towards the pier. We needed all the power the engine could muster to get us past and out into the open sea. There was another cough from the engine and our bows scraped the stone wall.

We had to turn back. Holding our breath, we made the turn with only inches to spare, relieved to feel the boat begin to steady herself again. But there was a great deal worse to come. Between the metal of the engine and the wooden planks of the deck we suddenly caught sight of a spurt of flame. The exhaust had come adrift and was belching red-hot gas into the bilges. There were forty gallons of petrol in the tank and we hoped against hope there had been no spillage. Our skipper was taking evasive action to clear the way for a tanker – a fair-sized vessel that was heading out of the harbour. As it turned, we saw the words of warning painted along its sheer sides in huge letters: FIRE. As though pat on cue, the petrol sloshing about in our bilges ignited and blazed up in a sheet of flame all round us.

We leapt out of the dog-house, ran to the forward hatch leading to the cabin, scrambled down the ladder, grabbed our life-jackets and some luggage, already packed, returned on deck and then, as flames crackled, jumped over the side.

Marianne was not a good swimmer but, with the help of the life-jacket, she put a healthy distance between her and the fire before she looked round. I had been in too much of a hurry to get away from the flames to secure my jacket properly and as I went down in a burst of bubbles, I saw it flapping away from me like an orange-coloured ray-fish. I can remember thinking that, having paid good money for the thing, it must be rescued. When Marianne glanced back, she saw me treading water and reaching for the jacket as it floated past. Behind me, fire had taken hold and was flaring dangerously near to the main fuel tank. Believing me to be in trouble, Marianne stopped swimming to shore and turned back. Her face was touched by the red flicker of the flames. I shouted to her that all was well but the noise from the fire muffled my voice. I tried waving at her but she, believing I was drowning, not waving, kept on swimming towards me with no regard for her own safety.

In the end, the three of us found ourselves being dragged from the water by willing hands. Our skipper trudged off wetly to find warm, dry clothing in his own boat which was still safely tied up at the jetty. But Marianne and I had nowhere to go and all we had in the world was aboard *Rona*. We turned to look at her, now an inferno, the flames leaping fifty feet into the air.

As we staggered up the beach, a total stranger took pity on us and invited us to stay with her for a few days while we found our bearings. Her house happened to overlook the sea-front and as we gazed from the bedroom window, we saw what little was left of *Rona* – now covered in white foam from a fire-tender drawn up alongside. Marianne turned to me with a look of horror and said, 'Oh God, the kitten!'

A few moments later, there was a knock on the front door. It was a fireman with a damp little bundle of fur. 'It might be alive', he said, without much hope in his voice. We called a vet, who diagnosed burnt lungs and gave us antibiotics which we administered in teaspoonfuls, mixed with milk. With tender loving care and medication, the kitten survived. (Later on, we gave it to my father who was looking for a cat to help keep down the vermin in the corn store attached to his shop.)

But that was the end of *Rona*. We were devastated. Looking out of the window and down at the crowd which had gathered to see our burnt-out boat, we began to realise just how severe a loss it was: above all, because we had forgotten to insure her.

Our hostess was like a fairy godmother. She helped us over the initial shock, preparing a steaming hot bath for us. We came downstairs in borrowed dressing gowns, to find her drying out our wet clothes; tea had been laid. We were about to sit down, when there was another knock on the door.

It was a local journalist. He didn't stay long. After asking us what we did and where we were going and what it was like to be shipwrecked, he left. We thought no more about it, merely expecting that our adventure might get written up in the local rag. Not so! The next day, *The News Chronicle* had given us a front page spread, together with a picture of *Rona* being hosed down. It read:

ACTRESS SWIMS FROM BLAZING BOAT: Firemen up to their waists in water, fight to save the cabin-cruiser. THREE – AND A CAT – ESCAPE. A young actress jumped overboard from a blazing cabin cruiser last night and swam fifty yards to safety…

We put aside all thought of looking for work in London and retreated to lick our wounds at my parents' house. By this time, they were living in an unremarkable semi-detached house on Macclesfield Old Road in Burbage, a part of Buxton. A short walk up the steep hill took us off the tarmac and on to the bumpy stones of an old Roman road leading towards wild moorland.

I found work taking young character parts in *Children's Hour* with the BBC in Manchester. It was during one of these productions that I was invited by David Scase, the director of the Manchester Library Theatre, to join his company. I was tremendously thrilled to be included in a cast with the actors Robert Stephens and Jeremy Brett. The standard of productions was very high. We had three weeks to rehearse each play – a luxury after weekly rep.

Marianne and I both wanted children but were content to wait until we had developed our careers. Nevertheless, we hadn't counted on what nature could get up to while we were unconscious. One night, after returning from Manchester and an exhausting day's work in the theatre, we woke up in the middle of the night – coupled.

We had made love in our sleep. We looked at each other in wonder, unable to believe that all that joy had been and gone without our knowing. Sleepily, Marianne murmured, 'I wonder who that's going to be.' And it *was* going to be somebody, because she was pregnant. The somebody was our first son, Richard. Later, when we told him how, by falling asleep, we had at the same time fallen deeper into the tender trap, he said he thought this was a very romantic way to be conceived. I am not sure he believed us.

Richard was born in Manchester Maternity Hospital on 19 November 1955. He took us both by surprise by arriving a week early. I had taken a job with *Children's Hour* at the BBC studios in Leeds and so missed the birth. Everyone in the cast sent Marianne flowers, including Violet Carson who later became famous as Ena Sharples, the old battleaxe in *Coronation Street*. At the time, she was playing a fairy princess to my fairy prince – remember, this was on radio. Not everyone had television in 1955, and radio actors still had quite a following. Having just heard me on the radio in a romantic part, the nurses and mothers in the ward were all agog to see me. I was a great disappointment: tired from the party of the night before and unshaven because I hadn't trusted my shaking hand, I staggered along the ward hoping I wouldn't cause any miscarriages. I found Marianne resting and happy, although she looked very fragile and worn out.

A Scots couple who lived in the flat above us lent us *Para Handy*, a book of comic short stories about the west coast of Scotland that I could read to Marianne during the night watches, to keep her company while she fed the baby. Here, had we known it, in these delightful little tales of Hebridean life, was an intimation of what lay before us.

Richard did everything to be expected of a healthy child. He was like clockwork with his feeds and very good-tempered. This meant that it wasn't long before we felt free to take him out with us in the evenings. The first time was to an end-of-production party at the Library Theatre. Marianne brought him to the stage door, carrying his nappies and powder in a suitcase. We put this on a work-bench in the scene-dock, just behind the stage. We had no carrycot so we put him in the suitcase, where he slept very peacefully with the lid propped open by a stage-brace. Every time we went backstage to make sure that all was well, we'd find a member of the cast with him, cooing and clucking.

Our second baby took his time coming into the world. One evening, when the child was already three weeks overdue, an actress friend, Alison Bailey, arrived bearing gifts as usual. She put down a bottle of red wine and cried out dramatically, 'It's high time that baby was launched. Drink that, my dear!' Marianne had Nicholas at home the next afternoon, 23 April 1958. It was a perfect delivery. He was floated in on the best Burgundy.

3

Alarms and Excursions

Suddenly, I found my career in Manchester taking off. ABC Television employed me as an assistant weekend announcer; *Children's Hour* was offering me more work than ever before; Granada Television used me on a regional magazine programme, *People and Places*; and they also engaged me as a voice-over in what was then a brand new show, *What the Papers Say*. Nevertheless, I still found gaps in my diary to accept parts as an actor in television drama.

We moved out of the flat and into a small house in a cul-de-sac. It was a quiet area and there was a garden where, when they were a bit older, the children would be able to play. After Nicholas had been weaned, Marianne went back to acting. She made commercials and Granada Television offered her the part of a public relations girl in a soap opera about an airport, starring Edward Woodward. Between us, we were now making some money and beginning to feel quite secure.

Then, one evening, Marianne returned from the studios announcing that she'd gone off coffee, hadn't wanted a cigarette all day and therefore must be pregnant again. Nowadays, her pregnancy might have been written into the script; but then, in the mid-1950s, her gradually expanding belly had to be hidden from the viewing public by a desk. She had to stay behind that desk at all costs.

Her third pregnancy became a strain on her back, so she left working for Granada; this was shortly before ABC Television closed down its Manchester studios. I was offered a job in Belfast but neither of us wanted to leave the mainland. All of a sudden, we found ourselves earning very little money, the result of rapidly reduced circumstances.

With Marianne six months' pregnant, I urgently needed to provide a steady income. It was Alison Bailey, our actress friend, who drew our attention to a line in the press advertising a modest job in Scotland.

I knew very little about Scotland. Like many English, I thought it was an eccentric extension of Tyneside. Neither of us had any romantic ideas about the country; indeed, we felt reluctant to move there. However, I put in an application for the job of Drama Adviser to the Scottish Community Drama Association and was successful.

'Troubles come not singly but in battalions'. Just as we were planning all these new excursions and putting them into action, we received a brave little letter from my mother. It was an alarm. She said we were not to worry, but Christie's, the big Manchester cancer hospital, had given her an appointment. At a time when my mother would have welcomed all of us near her, we were busy making arrangements to go and live even further north.

But it had to be done. To prepare for our arrival in Scotland, I left Marianne and the two boys in Manchester two months before the birth of the baby and went to look for accommodation in Edinburgh.

In Scotland, taking sides is a passionate national pastime and there is a strong partisanship dividing Glasgow from Edinburgh: if you like the one, it is a foregone conclusion that you dislike the other. I suppose I now side with Glasgow because it was to become our local metropolis. However, for one very important reason I still maintain a deep affection for Edinburgh: James was born there on New Year's Eve, 1960.

Marianne and the boys had arrived the week before. That day, as she went into labour, the streets of Edinburgh were littered with empty bottles, not a shop was open, and drunks incapable of getting themselves into the warm lay on the frosty ground like fallen statues. We didn't know what sort of a place we had come to. However, our Jewish landlord saw to it that we were well looked after, and when he heard I was to adjudicate drama festivals, he gave me his own dress suit which, because he was a tailor by trade, was especially beautifully cut. He gave it as a present 'for the baby'.

Marianne arranged to have another home confinement. Few other children were due in our part of the city, so the redundant midwives congregated in our flat. There were three of them in attendance when the contractions started. They sat on the bed, complaining that their work never gave them a chance to meet any men. Marianne, in considerable discomfort as a result of having met one, wondered why on earth they were so keen.

By this time, our domestic and professional situation was again very vulnerable. We had undergone radical readjustments: from rich to poor; from warm-hearted Manchester to cool, formal Edinburgh; from having friends to having none; from enjoying status in the television world to being virtually unknown. What's more, I had begun to lose my understanding of the amateur attitude to theatre. It was clear to me that some amateurs were far better actors than many professionals. Nevertheless, this did not affect my view that an amateur, no matter how good, fanned the flames; whereas a professional, no matter how bad, stepped right into the heart of the fire. There is a recognisable quality about a person ready to take the step from being an amateur to becoming a professional. During my stint with the SCDA, I only met one – and that was Bill Bryden. He left his Clydeside amateur club to become a brilliant director at the Cottesloe Theatre on the South Bank in London.

My job took me all over Scotland. I travelled here, there and everywhere. One day I would be lecturing a further education class in a Glasgow college. The next I would be in a little village in Fife adjudicating a festival of plays put on by the blind. The following week I might visit a prison for young offenders to take them through a rehearsal for a gang show. I would quite probably end up in Wick – or Skye where, with an architect, there would be a discussion about what was needed to turn a barn into a suitable venue for amateur productions. One eventful day, I was asked to go to Craignure, Salen, Dervaig and Tobermory on the Isle of Mull.

To reach Oban, the ferry port, I went by train from Glasgow through ninety miles

The three boys: Nicholas, 16; Richard, 18; James, 13

of magnificent country. On leaving the city, the broad River Clyde came into view and soon blurred the harsh edges of urban decay. Before long, all traces of city and river were gone and the train wound its way deep into the hills where, stretching into the distance, was Loch Lomond – pewter-grey, tree-fringed. The track climbed steadily. The ranks of thick conifers thinned out until only the toughest, most hardened veterans of the storms straggled the slopes. Each with an individual character, they crouched in grand isolation as if in readiness to take on anything the weather could hurl at them. Halfway to our destination, the train brought us under the high hills surrounding the village of Crianlarich where a huge eagle of rock appears to rise out of the ragged cliffs. It lours over everything, an ominous *genius loci*.

It was November. The early winter snows covered the higher ground and the clouds were torn by the mountain tops. It was a landscape designed by Gustave Doré . At times, I felt I was being presented with vistas that evoked the titles of paintingsin the romantic genre, *Sturm und Drang* or *The Valley of the Shadow of Death*.

When the train arrived in Oban late in the afternoon, the light was already failing and I could hardly make out the town. By morning, I saw it as a small conurbation determined to keep abreast of modern times but, thankfully, sufficiently slow in doing so to maintain an old-world charm. Oban is the regional market town, attracting people from miles around, including the island that was to become my home. It was from the old sea front that I first saw Mull: the mountains rose from behind the Isle of Kerrera and were so covered in snow clouds as to be barely visible. Their grey shape was that of a reclining woman, a Titanic siren sculpted by a giant Henry Moore.

I was to spend a week on the island. I boarded the ferry early and spent a few minutes watching the masthead gyrating slowly against the grey sky. Pale sunlight illuminated the whole panorama of peaks behind Oban: from the twin nipples of Ben Cruachan to the helmet-shaped Ben Nevis.

I went below to look for my guide, one Christie Park, the Youth Organiser for Argyll. I found him in the bar. He was kilted and dapper. The weather was bitterly cold. To prepare ourselves for disembarkation, leaving behind the warmth of the ship, we drank straw-coloured Glen Grant Whisky while he told me about the people I was going to meet.

In traditional folklore, Mull is the home of the Witch of Winter. It was she I must have seen reclining – massive, cold and forbidding. I cannot tell what spells she had laid upon the island in the past, but in present times, and for many years, she put a hex on television signals transmitted from the mainland. It took until the mid-seventies for three channels of television to be received generally. This was pertinent to my visit because I had actually come here to talk about television, to explain what people could expect of it once it did arrive.

Christie and I discussed what routes we should take in order to visit all the schools and village halls. I learnt from him that the island's entertainment was home-grown, with flourishing amateur drama groups in each of the main villages, whose connection with the outside world was mainly through *The Oban Times*, the radio and the Highlands and Islands Film Guild – a gallant concern, dedicated to bringing the latest films to the remote northern areas of Scotland.

I found Mull spectacularly beautiful. Unlike many parts of the Highlands, it is not overwhelming in its grandeur nor frightening in its isolation. It has upward of two thousand inhabitants and in shape – by a stretch of imagination – can be likened to a hand with the thumb pointing to the left. The fingers denote an area in the north where the hills are flat-topped and tilt in a distinctive way. The rock is black basalt and rivers grow old very quickly as they twist and tumble through it. The palm of the hand is where, many millions of years ago, there was gargantuan volcanic activity. Mountains rose to twenty thousand feet or more. Now, through the ceaseless effects of ice and snow, they stand at a modest three thousand, offering some of the finest scenery to be found anywhere in Britain. The thumb of the hand represents a granitic isthmus, pink and low-lying. It points to the sacred Isle of Iona, not much more than a stone's throw from the tip.

Much of the island is heavily wooded. A portion of the land owned by the Forestry Commission is given over to Sitka spruce. At the end of the branches of this beautiful blue-green tree are sharp spines that can catch the unwary and inflict terrible wounds to the eye. Otherwise, the variety of trees is extremely rich.

At the sea-fringe there are white sands in the north and black in the south. There are hills to climb, rivers to fish and paddle in, rocky coves to explore and, for the tough and well-booted, hundreds of square miles of heather to yomp over.

In 1961, as I looked at it through the porthole of the ferry, I could think only of the sleet and cold I was soon to brave. During the whole of this first visit, I was always slightly damp. I remember the guesthouse where a bedroom had been specially opened up for me. Normally, it was used only in the summer. A stone hot water bottle had been put in the bed to air it and as I slipped between the sheets, I was met by a cloud of steam. The bad weather continued throughout the week, but for me the fierce winds, the snow and ice, and glimpses of a dying sun enhanced the island's romantic mystery. It was as though the warm-hearted people, the scenery and dramatic weather were conspiring to entrap me. Most magical of all – and something I was never to see again – was the bewildering succession of rainbows. They were half-moon-shaped, star-shaped, and some were so truncated from the arc that they appeared to be square blocks of vibrant colour hovering in mid-air.

One mist-laden morning, Christie Park and I were driven from Tobermory in the north to Salen, a village lying some ten miles to the south. On this occasion, we'd left our own vehicle and were passengers in a car belonging to the Tobermory town clerk, now long since retired. We had come to a part of the road that runs beside a spur of sea lapping round a broken tooth of a ruin – Aros Castle. Without warning, the driver stopped the car, leaned across me, wound down the window, then, with the smoothest of actions, drew a rifle from beneath his seat, took aim and pulled the trigger. I was startled and deafened.

'Did you get him?' asked Christie.

'That I did not. The beast saw me and was away,' came the reply.

I was too stunned to ask questions. I had seen nothing – but was told that a stag had come down from the hills to find winter feed in the valley, presenting a likely target.

I returned home at the end of the week delighted with my first experience of Mull.

4

'And we in dreams...'

Early in the following year, I had been booked to adjudicate the island's Drama Festival. It was spring and the weather was perfect. The ferry was full of local people from Oban, also travelling to Mull for the Festival; and of course this was a good excuse for all of us to meet in the ship's bar as soon as we got on board.

In the early sixties the boat landed at Tobermory, which meant it had to make a twenty-five mile journey up the Sound of Mull. We were therefore fairly 'warm' by the time we arrived. I found myself being given VIP treatment. Having been met on the pier, I was then ushered straight to the Mishnish Hotel for more drinks. It was during this extraordinarily tipsy week that I realised that all the talk about how best to drink whisky matters not a tittle to the Highlanders. They are, in any case, the only true connoisseurs. 'There is no such thing as a bad whisky,' I was told. 'They're all good, but some are better than others.' To demonstrate this, I was offered a taste of this and that, then another, and another. Some were for the sweet palate; others, reminiscent of the smell of pulverised basalt, were better suited to those with jaded taste-buds. In turn, I savoured the aroma of smouldering peat, heather – and even of Ribena! 'Quite right, Mr Heskess...' ('th' sits uncomfortably on the tongue of the native Gaelic speaker). 'Quite right, you're drinking a Ribena Mac.' I was informed very seriously and with much nodding that 'Whisky is like a true Highlander – a friendly creature and a great mixer.' I found that it got into everything – coffee, tea, lemonade, Ir'n Bru (Scotland's other drink, the one that's 'made frae girders') and hot chocolate.

I ended up in such a state that I had to pour away my drinks behind the chairs and into potted plants or my wellies to save myself from an ignominious exit from the room. It was abundantly clear that, here on Mull, I was among the hard-drinking fraternity of the West of Scotland; there was no way I could compete.

The first night of the Festival ended with a parade of the drama groups and any member of the audience still capable of keeping upright. We marched down Tobermory Main Street led by a local piper. The evening was balmy and quiet and out in the bay a Fishing Protection Vessel had moored. In honour of the Festival, it had run out a string of lights from the masthead. Yachts bobbed gently, lights reflected in the water and, more or less in time to the fine skirl of the pipes, we swayed joyfully on our progress back to the hotel. So this, I thought, is what it is to be lionised!

The next day, Colin Morrison – the 'postie' from Dervaig – invited me to accompany him on his mail run that covered much of the north of the island. He was a small, keen-faced man with a deep voice and enchanting manners. His car was enormous. He used it as a post van, a taxi and as a small-scale lorry to carry vegetables and goods to local crofters and shops within his area. He opened a cavernous boot and showed me his supply of essential reserve petrol for topping up his gas-guzzler which, it seemed to me, he had to do every few miles.

We set off in the morning. The air was crisp and clear, giving a sight of the far-off mountains and sea the colour of Scots pine needles. I was quite prepared to believe the road turned upside down as it wound its tortuous course from Tobermory to Dervaig, seven miles distant. Every now and then, there were glimpses of the fairy isles of Tiree and Coll: they seemed to float above the sea which had now turned ice-blue. Following our arrival in Dervaig, we stopped for a while to meet various inhabitants and partake of a 'little something' – this always being a generous tumbler of whisky. I was introduced to a lady in need of help. An outdoor privy lay on its back in her garden and had to be got on to a local lorry, then transported to the next bay where she was preparing her cottage to accommodate summer visitors. Very politely, I was asked if I would give a hand with the lifting. We heaved it into place on the vehicle and left the carter to tie it down securely. We then continued down the road a couple of miles to Colin's home, a white-washed cottage at the site of the Old Mill. We stopped again for a cup of tea and another 'little something' supplied by his wife, Mary. 'It's cold the day!' I agreed, and was easily persuaded to take another wee drop to help us on our way to Colin's next port of call, which was at some dry-stone croft houses in the secluded bay at Croig.

Here, we caught up with the carter who was standing in the field by the road. He stood looking perplexed and scratching his head beside the privy that now lay on the grass, door face up. Colin and he exchanged a few sentences in Gaelic. Then he said, 'I'm afraid I'll have to ask you to give us a hand again, Barrie. The poor man has to get that thing up the track to the little croft – do you see, there?' He pointed way up a hill towards what looked like a heap of rocks topped by a pile of planks.

For the next half-hour we puffed and heaved up the stony track, dragging the privy as best we could towards the house. This was hard work without help. So we made a halt, deciding that it was time for another 'wee half'. Our footing became less sure – me in my nice new adjudicator shoes, the wellies having got too damp from the previous night's libations – as we sploshed through puddles and stumbled into cow-pats. These minor accidents gave us further excuses to stop, tell stories of similar adventures and encourage ourselves upwards and onwards with more 'wee drops'. When we fell over, we agreed that things were getting altogether out of hand and told a few more stories. We finally got the privy to its destination.

While the carter and I jiggled it to and fro, Colin took on the role of the user of the privy and instructed us as to the exact position from where he could sit and get the best view of the Cuillins of Skye, his wife's native home. We tried it out, admired the view, found it completely satisfactory and drank to our success. Skye was easy to see seventy miles to the north, and far out, in delicate pastel colours, shimmered the filmy islands of Harris and Lewis. It was a magical and happy day for me. And we in dreams – if somewhat alcoholic dreams – had beheld the Hebrides in all their splendour. The sea was liquid opal.

Coils of enchantment were wrapping round me.

The festival continued and, to my utter delight, the acting at its best matched anything the city drama clubs had to offer. The final night included two plays in Gaelic. A minister from the mainland had travelled to the island to be the Gaelic assessor.

Many of us, including the piper, had gathered on the pier to welcome him. Half an hour after he'd landed, he was leading the toasts in the bar of the Mishnish. I maintained my grip on sobriety by drinking only to the toasts I understood. That evening, in the crowded hall, the minister and I sat together at a little card-table placed in the central aisle. While I did my best to follow the story of the plays by watching, the minister was chuckling to himself between sups of whisky and muttering 'Och, Barrie, a fine Gaelic oath! What a pity it is you do not have the Gaelic. Och, ochone-ochone, a fine Gaelic oath!' He and the cognoscenti would hoot and yell their delight, stamping their feet, repeating the 'fine Gaelic oath' to each other until another exploded upon us, creating ever louder shouts of appreciation. The ancient electric stage lanterns were shaking in their fittings. To round off the occasion, speeches of congratulations, in Gaelic and English, were delivered from the stage.

The next morning we were joined on the ferry by a local schoolmistress. 'But what about the school?' I asked. 'Och, I've given the children a holiday. I am not missing the chance to talk drama and poetry.' While we drank to the memory of poets and playwrights, the festival continued unofficially on board the ferry. The minister was with us, but in spirit only. He was so deep in his cups that he took no part in the conversation. We said goodbye to our friends. Then Christie Park and I bundled the minister into the front seat of the car and drove off. We arrived at the minister's home but, getting no sign of life out of him, we opened his door and gave him an almighty push. He stood up, teetered, stepped forward, nearly fell flat on his face, got a leg in front just in time and then, without a word to us, tottered on his way up the drive to the manse. 'By God,' said Christie, 'I wouldn't like to be *him* waking up in the morn's morn. He'll be giving a hell of a hell-fire sermon on the evils of drink, mark my words!'

I returned to Edinburgh full not only of alcohol but of the enchantment of the world of Para Handy. Marianne said she had never seen a man look so green and yet so happy as I did when I staggered up the stairs to our flat.

That Sunday, we read in the press that a property on Mull, which we had noticed being advertised almost a year earlier, was again up for sale. We still didn't have the money to buy it but the pull of the island had begun to work on us. Furthermore, this was 1963. The two great world powers, the United States and the Soviet Union, were on a collision course. War was a distinct possibility. Having lived through the time when the atomic bomb was dropped on Japan in 1945, Marianne and I feared the worst, especially as we now had three children to think of. To our naive way of thinking, Mull offered an escape from disaster and all that we needed now was a twist of fate. It came.

The SCDA came to the conclusion that I was not cut out to work with amateurs and decided to dismiss me. At the very same time as I received my dismissal, the news came that my mother had died.

Her estate was larger than anyone had imagined and she left me the bulk of it.

Compared with what Marianne and I were used to, this represented a fortune. My mother had been fully aware that after her death my father would marry his cousin; and so, as though not wanting to facilitate their union, she did not leave him any of her money. For some time after this, I felt awkward with my father and we were to remain 'terribly English' about the whole affair. We never discussed it. Over the years, however, I realise that he was not resentful; on the contrary, he seemed glad for me.

With money behind us again, we felt freer than at any time since we'd left the studios; we did not fear for the future. We bought a second house in Edinburgh, not to live in but for letting. We invested in stocks and shares and found that Marianne had an eye for go-ahead companies. Our portfolio grew and became broad-based. It spread from the blue-chip market, which gave a small yield but promised steady and secure growth, through to a middle range of companies that were modest in growth and fairly reliable. Strictly for laughs, we included a few low-priced, high-risk companies such as diamond mines, which gave huge yields per year but only because threatened political upheavals promised no security whatsoever. Every morning we bought *The Financial Times* so as to plot the movement of the fifty or so companies we had invested in at any one time. We traced their progress in different coloured inks on a huge sheet of graph paper and knew exactly when to sell and when to buy in order to make a little profit.

With our affairs in good order, we looked again in the newspapers for something to buy on Mull. To our delight, the same property – a house called Druimard with an all-important outbuilding – was still for sale.

View from the Mull Little Theatre in winter

5

A Moving Episode

We were taking a family holiday near Lochgilphead, a small town in mid-Argyll and it was from here that we arranged to view Druimard for the first time.

It was a glorious day. The weather and the island were idyllic – or, as Para Handy might have said, 'chust sublime'. Masses of wild flowers trembled in the gentle breeze and the breeze itself smelled of honey. Far from being the home of the Witch of Winter, Mull was now host to the Spirit of Summer.

The drive from Salen Pier was up a long, dusty road that wound its way first through a little village and then a tunnel of shrubs and trees alongside the Sound. The scenery changed: the cosy prettiness of the coastal road gave way to a generous sweep of forest bordering the banks of the River Aros. We were then met by the basaltic table-top hills at the head of the River Bellart. The Bellart accompanied us in coils and ox-bows, shallows and narrow canyons before opening gently into a reed-covered loch. What we saw around us was evidence of powerful forces – fire and water and ice.

We were both excited and chattered on, as we always did, in a manner that was to earn us another nickname, 'Uncle and Antistrophe'. It was not the geological formations, however, which now preoccupied us so much as the promise of a new life for ourselves and our three sons. We began to plan.

For five years we would live on the income from letting one of the houses we owned in Edinburgh; with the sale of the other house, we would have enough money to buy Druimard. We would keep our needs to a minimum and the rent collected would, we thought, cover our requirements quite adequately. Then, when the boys were older and not so dependent on us, we would return to the mainland and re-enter the world of theatre. In the meantime, Mull offered us the right environment for doing other things. Marianne had already written stories and wanted to continue with writing a history of Shakespeare's times. I had sold several paintings in Edinburgh and here before me was an excess of subject matter… and the light!

The vehicle swung round a rocky corner in the road. Before us lay our promised land. I still think of it as a breathtaking view. To the west of the loch is a screen of pines and deciduous trees; water runs away under a little stone bridge to enter a narrow sea-loch. This is enfolded within two sloping arms of protecting hills between which, at the point where the loch runs into the Hebridean sea, there is a narrow strait where little islands float on the water and play games with perspective. On one of these islands is a perpendicular pencil smudge – a little, needle-shaped monument. Donald MacKechnie, the local road man, once said that it commemorated a certain MacNab who was 'unfortunately eaten by a lion in Africa'. That's what he told us…

We turned up a narrow dirt track that ran between tall pines and made a hairpin bend that brought us to the front door of Druimard. To our left was a tumbledown cow byre, so derelict that we hardly noticed it. We remarked in passing that it looked romantic. So were the tormentil-covered hill, the rings of mushrooms, the wild entanglements of blackberry bushes and the rowan trees protecting both the lower and upper parts of the garden from fairy spite. There was a fan of tall wych-elms to one side of the house and behind it were two of the most climbable beech trees one could ever wish for.

'We'll tell Nick and Rich they can have one each,' said Marianne. 'What about Jim?' I enquired. 'That's going to be a problem,' she answered. 'We'll face that one when he's old enough. We're bound to find a tree for Jim to climb when he's ready.' It was looking as though we had already made the decision to buy the house before we had even set foot in it: one isolated property sold to two wide-eyed innocents.

In a daze, we looked over the house. It was beautifully decorated. There were lots of rooms, large and airy, and the stairwell was open and attractive. The building had been a manse and, before the First World War, the home of a Free Church minister, the Reverend Paterson and his wife. Since then, it had been inhabited by a family of old ladies and, if the bottles I was later to find lying hidden in great numbers under the garden walls were anything to go by, they must have been ladies with a very healthy capacity for the hard stuff.

'We'll have to get a car, Barrie. We can't live here without one.' I had taken driving lessons in Edinburgh and, a fortnight before we left for Mull, had failed my driving test by making a complete hash of a hill start. But for now, we were confident we'd both be driving within a few months. The owner of Druimard told us that, until we got our own transport, we could shop in the village. He drove us the quarter mile to the top of the one main street and introduced us to the lady who ran the post office, Nelly. We then met Johnnie, a wizened little man with rheumy eyes who ran the general store. It was an amazingly gloomy shop – so dark, that it was impossible to see what you were buying. There was a rack of fifty or more blackened little drawers set on the wall behind a grimy counter. These drawers held minute quantities of goods for sale: tobacco twist, dried peas, matches, cotton, needles, candles and oil wicks. They brought back memories of my father's shop. Johnnie, gnome-like, shuffled out of an ill-lit room at the back and greeted us very politely. We noticed that when he served customers, he did so extremely slowly, rather like a clockwork toy in the process of winding down. Indeed, shortly after we came to live on Mull, he wound down altogether and his shop was sold and modernised.

That night we stayed at the Western Isles Hotel in Tobermory, having decided to sleep on whether or not to buy the house. Next morning, sunlight burst into the room. We looked at each other across the pillows. Marianne's eyes were big – bigger than usual. She was wide awake. 'Shall we?' she asked. I held my breath for a second or two, then said, 'Yes!'

We now had two houses to furnish, the recently purchased house in Edinburgh as well as Druimard. The furnishings in our Murrayfield flat were sufficient to fill four modest-sized rooms. The difference between what we could fill and what we needed

Druimard, 1970s

to fill was twelve rooms. What was more, the children would have to have suitable clothing for the country; and food stores would depend on buying monthly rather than daily, deep-frozen rather than fresh. We soon found that there was nothing better guaranteed to dispel the euphoria occasioned by the purchase of an island property than facing up to the logistics of the move. Nevertheless, we were riding too high on excitement to consider that what we had done might be foolhardy. God was in His heaven and all was right with the world.

The moment we committed ourselves to the purchase, the list-making began. This caused a twinge of nostalgia. My mother had owned a Victorian aide-memoire which she had inherited from her mother and was still using to make shopping lists in the 1950s. It was made from oblong leaves of ivory, the size of visiting cards. Pinned together by a silver stud at one end, they could be made to fan out. You could easily mark them with a pencil and when a list became redundant, it could be erased by rubbing firmly with the finger. I seem to have watched women making lists right through my life; often, when another piece of paper is brought out of a handbag and consulted, I am reminded of those elegant ivory leaves.

Mr MacIntyre – known locally as Angus the Bank – had arranged that we should visit John Stevenson, an Oban solicitor. We came away from his chambers reassured that we had done entirely the right thing. Both he and Angus had an attitude to doing business that was undeniably sound but unlike anything we had experienced in the city. The bank manager offered us generous shots of whisky, poured from a bottle kept in his desk, whilst telling us about the 'other' bank and of the rivalry between them. The solicitor interwove hard facts and sensible advice with anecdotes about local characters and boating adventures. At first we suspected that this was all a ploy to spin out the time, for which we would later be charged; on the contrary, this was the Highland way of conducting transactions. There is a hoary joke: for the Gael, the Spanish word for tomorrow, 'mañana', has an awful feeling of urgency about it. However, he is not so slow that he cannot expedite matters when required. Arrangements had also been

Dervaig village, 1960s

made for me to see a local doctor for a routine check on my health so that we could raise a mortgage.

Dr McIntyre had a shock of white hair and piercing blue eyes; he was like a short length of animated wire. I accepted a large glass of whisky from him and then we got down to business. His daughter, a keen knitter, had borrowed his inch-tape and so he measured me round the chest using a hank of garden twine that he pulled out from under his desk. To assess my girth, he held the twine against the height-gauge standing in the corner of his surgery. It took us some time to work out what, at first, neither of us could understand: how I came to have a chest measurement of nearly six feet.

Later, I learnt from other islanders that when the doctor was on his rounds, any passenger he happened to have with him was asked to sit in the back seat because his first wife, who had died several years previously, had first claim on the front seat beside him. I was also told that when he travelled between Dervaig and Croig he would open and shut his car door at certain points along the route to give a lift to an itinerant ghost. Such were the local stories about Dr McIntyre, although personally I never witnessed this side of him.

On the return ferry, a piper in full Highland fig was playing. The crystalline rocks, luxurious trees and blue mountains of Mull slid gently away on our starboard side. The sea breeze whipped the music hither and thither and, not for the last time, we were enthralled by the magic of the Hebrides.

As soon as we returned to the holiday cottage, we were met by a barrage of questions from the excited boys. Were there any sweetie shops? Where was the school and what was it like? How many trees were there? Could they make as much noise as they liked? Were there deer and otters? And could we have a cat? Could they have an otter? Could they have one each?

It became increasingly clear that, at least from the point of view of the children, we had not made a mistake in buying the property. All the same, it would have been prohibitively expensive to furnish all the rooms in our two new houses, had it not been for the Edinburgh lane sales. These were held every week in the open air at the back of the auction rooms, where items of low value were bought and sold. In every sale of this kind there used to be job lots. In Lot 79 there was a box containing a bundle of old red velvet. 'Very useful curtaining,' we had thought at the time, and put it away without really looking at it. Little did we know.

I arranged for a local family firm to organise the move. One day in August 1963, they came and packed all our belongings into a large pantechnicon. Richard, Nicholas and I, according to strength and ability, carried the suitcases and bags containing our overnight things. Marianne took James – still just a toddler – and together we set out for the train. The pantechnicon was to meet us at Oban. Here, we expected the load to be manhandled on to a small motor-driven boat that we would then join for the trip to Tobermory. Once there, everything was to be transferred to a local lorry and taken to Druimard – simple! Foreseeing that we just might be too tired on the first night to organise the move into the house, we had arranged with the Balfour Pauls, a local landowning family, to spend the night in their bothy, a small cottage situated in a copse a mile across the valley from our new home.

We left Glasgow and were soon at Bowling, where we caught a glimpse of the Clyde between the fanning branches of trees and shrubs lining the railway. The river lay at the turn of the tide, oily and sullen. Turning away to look out of the windows on the other side of the carriage, the boys shouted and pointed at the flocks of geese guarding the bonded warehouses. Curls of steam and smoke drifted past the window-pane.

Whisky in bond and oil in huge tanks, trees stretching upward and fuel pipes running sideways – a crude metal weft piercing a delicate, sylvan warp. The river widened rapidly. On the opposite bank sprawled the shipbuilders' yards of Greenock and Gourock. Large ships waited monumentally, ready to be launched. 'There – a sub, d'you see Dick? Where I'm pointing, Nick, there!' While James slept in his mother's arms, his brothers hung on the thick leather strap which was part of the window fastening and gazed at the black fin cutting the water. Little did they know that an important element in our decision to leave the central industrial belt of Scotland was the threat of nuclear war.

As we hauled up beside Loch Long we saw the Highlands, still a distant outline of gentle curves. The train climbed steadily. I told Nick, aged four and a half, the song of the train as it went up a gradient: 'I think I can, I think I can, I think I can.' Then, as the track levelled out and the going got easier: 'I thought I could, I thought I could, I thought I could.' It wasn't long before we looked down on sleek warships, grey cranes towering over them, their baleful, red eyes glinting at the pulley-heads. We passed Garelochhead and came to banks of gently waving willow-herb, shrubs and the branches of trees which swooshed and snapped against the carriage window and made us jump.

At last we were among the high hills. At their foot and climbing half way up their sides, there were ranks of conifers, green-clothed giants looking down over the loch. The edges of the hills were now close enough for us to discern every tremble in the outline: the hand that had drawn it was shaky – frightened by its own creation. The air had cleared and there was not a cloud to be seen. The sky was iridescent blue, the hills emerald, the rocks brown, the loch ultramarine. The reflections formed a deep-coloured tartan.

By the time we rattled and shook round the curve of the track approaching Oban, the children were tired. They soon revived when they realised that at last they were free to explore the unfamiliar things they found along the pier – the bollards, coils of thick ropes and gangways. The little boat was tied up as we had expected and lay at a good height for transferring our belongings. But there was no pantechnicon in sight. Time went by, the tide receded, the deck sank with it. The owner of the vessel checked his watch.

The weather remained calm, though clouds had begun to form and rain threatened. The deck was slipping lower and lower. The skipper warned us that it would soon be impossible to lift down much of the heavy stuff, if and when it arrived. In any case, because night was approaching, it would soon be too dark for anything to be done at all. At long last, with forty minutes to spare, the lorry arrived. We hurriedly unpacked what we could and handed it down into the hold. As we worked, we were told the reason for the delay. A long wheel-based crane had tried unsuccessfully to circumnavigate a humpback bridge at Inveraray, and had become lodged half-way across. With all its wheels off the surface of the road, it had rocked backwards and forwards, immobilised, blocking the main route to Oban for miles back. Our driver had been forced to make an enormous detour along the narrow highland roads.

Before long, only the lightest of the goods could be handed down to the men in the boat. It was decided to leave everything else on Oban Pier and set off for Tobermory while there was just enough light to navigate. Unused to the innate honesty of the Highlander, we were anxious about leaving anything behind.

Richard and Nicholas were each allowed a turn at the ship's wheel. Marianne sat on the deck with James. The skipper gave us hot, strong tea laced with condensed milk to keep out the cool evening air. We watched the serrated range of mountains behind Oban becoming mistier and mistier as the sun went down. Nicholas dozed off, resting his head on his mother's arm. Richard chattered on about what he was seeing and what he hoped to see. Then, suddenly, there was an electrifying moment: a dolphin-like creature rose majestically from the wine-dark sea, not thirty yards from the boat. It stood on its tail for a long second, before smacking down with a thunderous splash. Porpoises, clerical grey, smooth and glistening, swam all around us.

The weather suddenly turned unpleasant and it began to rain hard. Four hours later, tied up at Tobermory Old Pier, we started the business of lifting the furniture up the steep rock wall. We stacked it as best we could by the light of the single electric bulb that hung, dripping, from a rusty stanchion. The lorry-driver who was to have met us had gone home. The children had been wonderfully good the whole long day; but they were now looking pale and wanting their beds. So, while I stayed back to complete the unloading, Marianne and the boys took a taxi out to the bothy. Several hours later, I joined them. I slept deeply that night. I was past caring that most of our possessions had been left in two unguarded, sorry lots – one in Oban and the other in Tobermory – getting drenched by what I've heard described as 'torrential Highland drizzle'.

6

Swings and Roundabouts

There are moments when time seems to stand still and there is no proper sense of space or season: one is in the world, but not of it. We experienced this kind of dislocation particularly keenly on New Year's Eve 1963, our first such celebration on Mull. The children were in bed, asleep. We had prepared and cooked a venison pie and eaten it by candlelight. Then we went out into the garden; the night air was uncannily warm and, except for the sound of a distant waterfall, everything was hushed. We raised our glasses, golden with Drambuie, to drink the midnight toast. There we stood, as though protected by the tall, dark trees. It was easy to believe that the peace around us flowed out beyond to embrace the whole world – and that it would go on like this.

However, there was to be a rude awakening. By April, it became clear that all was not well. Living far from our property in Edinburgh and unable to keep a close watch on the stock market – *The Financial Times* was not delivered to the island – our material circumstances took a sudden and dramatic downward turn. The agent who had looked after our interests in Edinburgh, and this included collecting the rents from the house, was arrested and sent to prison; a number of his clients – and we were amongst them – had been relieved of a significant portion of their investments. We sold the house in Edinburgh, but even so our financial position deteriorated to such a low level that for a fleeting moment we thought we might have to sell Druimard as well and leave the island. The prospect of returning so soon to the mainland fired our pride. The alternative to painting pictures, writing books – and failing – was to let rooms, run a guesthouse and do our best to succeed.

In our enthusiasm to make a go of the new venture, we over-capitalised, thereby compounding the problem. The furniture I had bought in the Edinburgh lane sales was hardly enough to see us through the first season of letting a few rooms. Comments from our guests, though politely phrased, made it clear that there would have to be changes. But in purchasing new beds and bed linen, tables, chairs, cutlery and kitchen utensils, and making small but essential structural alterations to the house, our resources were fast whittling down to dangerously low levels. Then came a further shock. Greenhorns that we were, we hadn't taken into account how very isolated Druimard was: we were well off the main tourist route on the island. There was a dearth of passing trade. The little money we had saved from the Edinburgh fiasco soon went and we were now in the red.

Nevertheless, there was a little light, a faint glimmer to lift our flagging spirits. The few guests that we did attract were treated to a very good service. The meals we offered were custom-designed to suit the palate of each individual guest. On one occasion, a lawyer who specialised in ticket-fraud, had mentioned a predilection for gazpacho.

Because he was due to leave us the following day – before lunch – Marianne promised him he would have a bowl of his favourite soup for breakfast. Marianne's cooking got us into *The Good Food Guide*.

It was at about this time that the man from the 'Hydro-Electric' who used to come and read the meter, asked us outright, 'Exactly how much did you pay for this property, Mr Hesketh?' Under other circumstances, I would have told him to mind his own business. However, there was such an air of candid friendliness about the enquiry that I told him straight, knowing that whatever I said, the sum would inevitably get graded up or down, depending on who was telling whom around the island.

'Four thousand nine hundred pounds,' I answered. 'Well, I hope it's all right for you!' he replied. I told him that I thought it was. 'Well, I hope so,' he said, and left.

Was this an example of natural Celtic pessimism or did he have information that we didn't? Soon after, we found out that Druimard had been renovated by the same person who had sold a similar property – three miles up the road towards Calgary – to Rab Butler, the parliamentarian. That house was said to have leaking pipes and collapsing ceilings. Although our problems were not of this order, we certainly did have trouble with Druimard.

During our first year of letting bedrooms we lived in the main house. Not only was this a strain on the family, but it meant we inhabited bedrooms that could otherwise be let. So, with a loan from the Highland Fund, we bought materials to put up a summer cottage and then built it ourselves. Except for cladding the roof, Marianne and I did everything. We laid the foundations, put up the walls, fitted the windows and wired the building for electricity. From the start, the boys always referred to it as 'the hut'. It stood between the tumbledown byre and Druimard itself. During the summer tourist season we moved into it as a family and immediately felt the benefits.

Nevertheless, Mull remained a marginal holiday resort and therefore hypersensitive to changes in the British economy. We could not help being nervous about the future.

One day, as we were standing at the kitchen window, looking across at the old byre, Marianne wondered aloud, 'What shall we do with it? How can we make it earn us some money?' Although we considered the situation very carefully, at this point we did not think, 'Empty building plus two actors equals theatre.' Our minds were taking another path: we would turn the byre into a little café and shop.

We were soon setting to work again and building shop-counters out of old plywood. We painted them a miserable grey – the only colour we could afford in a sale of paint at a local store. 'They'd make nice stage rostra,' said Marianne, turning one over and standing on it. We didn't pursue the subject, shrugging it off as an impossible dream.

Over the next year, we stocked our shop with sale-or-return good-quality woollens and offered excellent home-made soup in the café, but the venture was not a great success. On the other hand, the guesthouse remained popular: visitors kept on coming, enjoying their stay and we made many friends. There were of course moments when we found ourselves exasperated and amused at the same time.

One marvellous September evening, late in the tourist season, we faced a minor disaster. There were twenty guests in the house for dinner. We knew that, after coffee had been served and drunk, there would be a call on the lavatories and that in no time at all a hundred gallons of water would be flushed through the plumbing system. Suddenly, in the middle of doing the washing up, the water supply failed.

I ran two hundred yards up the hill to where our small private reservoir was situated. There was nothing wrong there; it was full and the spring was bubbling. I reported back to the kitchen. There was nothing we could do except delay serving the coffee and pray for a rain storm to fill up our supply of buckets. However, the sky was becoming velvety and looked set to continue the fine spell of weather we had been enjoying. Like an enormous globe, the golden moon shone through the leaves of the beech tree behind the house. Suddenly, from out of the shadows, stepped the plumber. I hadn't phoned for him; he just materialised – happened to be there. I nearly fell on his neck for joy. I told him about our predicament.

'Bring a spade, Mr Hesketh, and have you a knife, a nail, a piece of wood and a hammer?' I went to get what he asked for. When I returned, he was standing under the beech tree. 'Your spring rises over yon hill, am I not right? And is there water in the tank?' he asked.

'There's plenty of water; it's brimming over.' 'Very well.' He pointed. 'The pipe will come this way, under the wall, following that dip in the land. So it should run along here.'

Whereupon, from the pockets of his overalls, he whipped out what at first sight I took to be two very slim revolvers. But, as the leaves rustled and parted, casting a mottle of shadow over us, I saw that they were twisted lengths of copper wire, bent at right-angles. He held them – like revolvers – in front of him. It was a bizarre sight: this tall, thin man, framed in the moonlight, walking slowly over the rough ground grasping ethereal six-guns. Suddenly, they leapt in his hands as if he had fired off a couple of rounds.

'Dig there!' he commanded. I set to with a will, motivated by the thought of twenty full bladders craving imminent relief. The spade struck rock. 'That will be the ground water that activated my wee sticks,' he said. 'We'll try a bit farther.'

On we walked, he with his divining-rods and I with my spade. There was another violent twist from the bent wires and again came the order, 'Try there!' This time, I dug deep into the soil – deep, that is, by Mull standards. Usually rock is hit within the first three inches. I went down six, then struck something that gave out a dull, hollow sound.

'That's it. Now, will you take that piece of wood you have with you and sharpen it to a point – a thin, thin point.' While I whittled, he scraped at the pipe with the spade and, producing a torch, knelt to gaze at the lead snaking dully through the earth. 'Would you put the nail there,' – he pointed to the top of the pipe – 'and give it a wee bit bash wi' yon hammer!' I did as I was told. The nail sank easily into the soft lead. 'Now pull it out.' As I withdrew it, the lead snake I had just wounded breathed a long sigh, a sigh that went on and on until it was stopped by a bubble of water that grew and rose into a fine fountain six feet high, wetting me and the ground all around.

'That'll do it, Mr Hesketh.' With the air-lock cleared, the water flowed through the system again. I then understood what the wooden stick was for: to bung up the hole made by the nail and so stop the spurt of water.

Eventually, our private water supply broke down altogether and we were joined to the mains piped from the reservoir in Dervaig. Over the years, Marianne, my sons and I had often been on the hill to search for the pipe. We got adept at tracing its whereabouts with bent copper wires, then digging through the turf and knocking in nails to relieve the air-locks. We would imitate the plumber as we worked: 'Now Richard, plug the hole with your wee bit stick. Knock it in wi' yon hammer. Give it a wee tap!' And we'd laugh at the pun.

Neither Marianne nor I had any opportunity to consider the deeper meaning afforded by the experience, its metaphorical significance rich in Jungian imagery: earth, water, metal, snake, moon. That was lost on us at this time. There was no tranquillity in which to recollect and appreciate the poetic side to our lives. The exigencies of each day – getting and spending – demanded that we only look outward, mostly towards satisfying the requirements of our guests.

There is something about September that seems to bring out the best and worst in the tourists. We could not help noting that the month of mists and mellow fruitfulness had a way of revealing people – like characters in melodrama – in true, strong colours, warts and all. By the end of the season we found ourselves too emotionally exhausted to cope easily with such people. As for your dyed-in-the-wool eccentrics, we couldn't handle them at all – that is, without help.

There was one particular lady who threatened to drive everybody to distraction, ourselves and the rest of the guests included. She was middle-aged, thin and haggard-looking. She had travelled up from the south of the island, twenty-five miles in a local taxi. The taxi-driver warned me, 'She's done nothing but carry on all the way up, I don't envy you having her in the house – you'll get nothing but trouble from her. I've seen that type before.'

The woman was obviously deeply unhappy and complained about everything: the food, the bed, the isolation and the other guests, who were very forbearing. When she wasn't complaining, she was weeping in the corner of the living room. And when she wasn't doing that, she poked around in every nook and cranny. If she found the bathroom engaged, she would turn off the light switch outside, leaving the occupier in total darkness. She was a character in search of a play.

As chance would have it, we happened to have a psychiatrist staying with us at the time. One morning, I approached the doctor after a tense breakfast (at which the woman had been particularly objectionable to everyone), and asked for any suggestions about how to cope with her.

The answer came pat, 'Be firm. Look her in the eye, tell her that you have noticed that she is unhappy here and that you have ordered a taxi to take her through to Tobermory, where she will find a hotel to her liking. It is important that you pay for the taxi and impress upon the driver that it is your hire, not hers. Tell him that halfway to his destination, probably when he is opposite the Mishnish Lochs, the woman will ask him to return here. He is to ignore her and continue to Tobermory. As you explain to the woman what arrangements you have made for her, she will start to cry. You must keep looking at her and tell her you have no sympathy for her whatsoever. The tears will dry up.'

I carried out the instructions very carefully. On cue, the woman started to weep as the doctor had said she would. I stopped her to order and the tears all but climbed back up her cheeks into her eyes. The next time I saw the taxi-driver, he looked at me in wonder and said, 'How did you know that woman would ask me to turn round at the Mishnish Lochs?' 'It was just a feeling I had,' I said.

Among the late-season guests, there was one very memorable family comprising grandfather – a Vice Admiral – his lady and two small girls, their grandchildren. The old man was full of charm. He told us he had been hit on the head by shrapnel whilst serving in the Navy in the Mediterranean and that we were not to be alarmed if we found him wandering at night: the wound had left him with a propensity for sleep-walking. True to his word, he once came into our bedroom, fast asleep but with his eyes wide open, asking to be shown his granddaughters. We went along the landing to their room where, at his request, I turned on the light. Seeing them sleeping safely, he nodded and, still asleep himself, let me guide him back to his own bedroom. There he was greeted by a tremendous shout from his lady, as if from the poop deck in a storm, 'Where have you been, you silly old salt?'

There was another September family – a fearfully pompous woman who came with her daughter and husband; but since it seemed that he preferred to camp out under canvas in the garden and we saw little of him, he plays no part in the story.

The girl was fifteen, physically mature, attractive and intelligent. But her mother simply refused to let her grow up and treated her like a child of four. On one occasion, the woman addressed us all with great satisfaction, emphasising how much her daughter depended on her, the mother: 'She's such a little one… Don't sit like that, darling, you're showing everything you've got! Isn't she sweet?' Then, turning back again to her daughter, she asked rhetorically, 'And what would you do without your Mummy?'

Everyone else, feeling sorry for the girl, behaved towards her like the young woman she really was. And of course this put the cat among the pigeons. What with mother pulling one way and the world pulling the other, the resulting split was too much for the girl. One afternoon, I came into the hall to find her in a catatonic state, unable to move and hardly breathing. Marianne called the doctor, who drove up immediately, made an examination and, as she went to the kitchen to phone for the ambulance, said, 'On no account let that mother near her daughter!' Once the family had left, we never heard anything more about them.

Possibly the oddest September guest was the person who was convinced that the world's youth were under the control of a criminal locked up in San Quentin Penitentiary. To save the young people of the locality from his malign influence, she pulled all our telephone wires out of the wall.

The café had been a failure and the guesthouse may not have rewarded us with any financial security. But it did present us with an extraordinary pageant. It was a form of theatre in which we, the servants, were also the audience. Slowly but surely a pattern was forming; fate was guiding us inexorably towards the creation of the Mull Little Theatre.

7

The Thursday Theatre

One morning in autumn, after all the guests had left for home, Marianne, sitting in a bedroom overlooking the byre, initiated the all-important conversation. 'Is there something – anything – we can offer our guests other than food and a bed? There's very little to do in the evenings, especially if you're a fishing widow.'

We looked at each other, and then at the byre. 'It's very small – but…' I said. 'Well,' said Marianne, not waiting for me to finish, 'Shall we have a look?'

We walked over to the little basalt and wooden building which, up until now, had housed our shop and café. We stared round at the dark, rough walls and split-level floor. I nodded towards the raised part and remarked that it could be the stage. 'No,' replied Marianne, 'the audience must be higher than the actors. Audiences like to look down on their gods!'

I strode out the length and breadth: it was twenty-eight feet by fourteen. Not very long, not very wide, but big enough for a box of delights. A playbox.

And so, without even mentioning the word 'theatre', without any fuss, the idea for the Mull Little Theatre was born.

We returned to the house. 'Barrie, let's get out that velvet we bought in the sales. It looked like curtaining.' I had stashed it away in the loft – a loft that was to hold many theatrical secrets in future. At first I couldn't find it but eventually managed to lay my hands on the bundle. I brought it down to Marianne. She began unwinding ecstatically. 'Oh, my! Is all this meant? It's a pelmet – a wine-coloured pelmet and it's *huge*. It must have been used in a theatre once upon a time!'

We were in the hallway, sitting back on our heels and looking at this new-found treasure. There it lay, cut to fit some other, unknown proscenium arch. It seemed to be inviting us to use it again. We felt a frisson of pleasurable anticipation. It was then that Marianne coined the phrase, 'Thespis Aid Us', which invocation she always used before stepping out on stage. At one time, she nearly convinced me that there might be a future in selling bottled sugar-water in the foyer labelled 'Thespisade'.

Working on the byre and turning it into a theatre was like a homecoming. We set about what we had to do, fully aware that it might not – indeed probably would not – work. But, what the hell, we were in our element.

The enthusiasm that welled up with the discovery of the pelmet was absorbed into the serious business of adapting the building. As we discussed and planned, measured and cut, constructed and painted, the excitement that had swept over us like a wave returned more gently, like a rising tide, slow and steady. We shared an absolute conviction about what we were doing. It was fortunate for us that the byre was so small; we made everything ourselves, exactly as we wanted it.

The byre in its original state

The byre, work in progress

As the news spread about our venture, friends began donating things. One of these gifts was a fine set of curtains that we hung round the back of the stage. We allowed ourselves an acting area ten feet wide; it took all of two good strides to cover the distance from the front to the back.

I designed a set of swinging arms from which other curtains could be hung and moved like Japanese screens, thereby opening and closing small perspectives which, in turn, gave a variety of entrances and exits. Inspiration for this simple device had come from several sources: the Sir John Soane Museum in London, which demonstrated how much can be made of small spaces; memories of Jean Cocteau's film sets – all mirrors, screens and imaginative vistas; shoebox theatres that I'd made as a child; and the recollection of being taken by my parents to pantomimes in Birmingham, whose extravagant and vast sets had many openings and closings for the comics to disappear into and pop out of unexpectedly.

The stage lighting was improvised. In those days, paraffin was in great demand on the island and used to be carted about in five-gallon cans. The Tobermory shops sent vans round the villages stocked with household good and foodstuffs but, because of the tainting smell, none of them would carry paraffin. Only the bank van would accept it. We collected several of these cans which, being about two feet high and eighteen inches in diameter, could easily be adapted to serve as theatre lanterns, not dissimilar to the professional lantern then known as a 'bomb'. Inside, they were shiny with oil and reflected a hundred-watt bulb quite adequately. Cutting out one of the ends was a five-minute job, and fixing a bulb holder at the other end hardly took longer. As the proscenium arch was only ten feet high, these lanterns could hang near enough to the actors to cast quite a strong light and still be out of sight of the audience.

To begin with, there were no dimmers. Our lighting was very basic, just a matter of switching on and off. Before we bought some simple professional apparatus to control the lighting effects, we made six dimmers by cobbling together blocks of lead attached to pieces of string, which in turn were tied to wooden levers, themselves suspended over Kilner jars filled with brine. These contraptions worked remarkably well; just sometimes they would give trouble and heat the water to boiling point, in which case we would give them a kick to make the connection through clouds of turbulent liquid and lead precipitate. I was sorry to see them go – they fitted the general rusticity of the venture. But they were not safe.

This was the time when one of the Hydro-Electric engineers turned up to mend a fault in the line to the theatre building. He was standing on a chair and, pausing to consider my stage lighting, he suddenly lost concentration, wielded his hammer and hit his thumb. 'Och, that nail bloody!' he cried out. He turned to apologise for his language, 'Sorry, Marianne, but in the Gaelic we always put the adjective after the noun!'

We had very soon learnt that it was inadvisable to rely on electrical power alone. So, to be on the safe side, we kept a reservoir of Calor gas to heat a small double-ring stove in the kitchen. A lady from the village who used to help us in the guesthouse brought her daughter with her at the weekends and during school holidays. Pat was an engaging fifteen-year-old who was studying for O-level English. Marianne took her through the examination texts, one of which was *Macbeth*. One cold winter evening, she was sitting with us going over the speech by the 'Bloody Sergeant'. When we came to the lines '… The merciless Macdonwald[1]… from the Western Isles/ Of Kernes and Gallowglasses is supplied…' she stopped us and said, in wide-eyed wonderment, 'I didn't think they had Calor gas in them days!' Another time, when we asked her about what she was doing at school, she had said, 'Oh, there was this po-yem about a wee, weird, weary man with a pelican hung round his neck.' In her own poetic way, she was referring to Coleridge's *The Rhyme of the Ancient Mariner*.

Apart from our supply of 'gallowglasses', we also used a Rayburn that burnt smoke-less fuel. There were the open hearths which took logs, and in every room we placed paraffin heaters. Lighting was backed up by Tilley lamps and dirty but attractive glass-chimney lamps and plain, no-nonsense candles. We learnt to develop a siege mentality; winters in the Highlands and Islands can be very dreich – long and trying, without heat or light.

Back in the theatre, whether hanging the lanterns, switching them on and off, all together or in sequence, or standing on stage pulling the curtain cord and trying out a speech, our hearts were filled with confidence – not in the future, but in the building as a theatre. We felt the magic. This time we knew we were doing the right thing.

It was time to turn our attention to the auditorium. We now had new beds for the guesthouse and the old ones, bought in Edinburgh, were stacked and ready to be taken to the rubbish dump at the north end of the village. I saved them just in time. By cutting, bending and bracing, I made half a dozen crude, settee-like frames to which I lashed the original mattresses. They proved extremely comfortable seating for thirty people: although home-made, it would probably have remained the most luxurious in any British theatre, except that they took up too much space. Later on, we replaced the bed-settees with a consignment of tip-up seats from a dismantled cinema, plus six fauteuils. These last were ordered at an opportune moment: whilst measuring out the flour for a batch of cakes, we noticed that our catering suppliers were offering one comfortable chair for every ten tokens off their bags of flour.

Eventually the time came when we felt the theatre was all but complete. We stood outside and congratulated ourselves. Then we noticed that there was something missing over the big wooden door.

'Isn't there usually a sign over the entrance to concert halls and theatres, to the effect that they are licensed for public performance?' Marianne agreed with me that there usually was. I wrote to the county clerk of Argyll and Bute to ask what, if anything, we should do. We heard nothing. Several weeks later, I phoned him.

'And will you remind me what it is you have in mind to do in this theatre, Mr Hesketh?'

'Put on a play,' I answered.

---

1 *The Arden Shakespeare*, I.ii.9

'There'll be nothing immodest?'

'Good heavens, no.'

'I'll have to look into it. In the meantime I'll put your enquiry in the pipeline.'

'So it will be all right, then?' I asked anxiously, 'We can go ahead with putting on a show?'

'Well,' came the thoughtful reply, 'You're an awfu' awfu' long way away.'

The enquiry remained in the pipeline for all the years Marianne and I ran the Mull Little Theatre.

In 1966, there was an all-out shipping strike that threatened the livelihood of the thousands of people who lived on islands round the whole of Britain. The strike lasted for six weeks during the height of the tourist season. Those who did visit Mull were ferried in private leisure boats from Oban. Instead of the usual crowd of visitors, the island received only small groups of ten or twenty. This was the year we chose to open the Little Theatre.

We were given a slight advantage when the newly inaugurated government agency, the Highlands and Islands Development Board, floated a rescue operation for those of us in a particularly vulnerable position. We were teetering on a knife-edge and it was fortunate that we were just within the limits set by the Board for aid. Their donation did at least keep closure at arm's length; but no more. There was no black, only red, deep red on our bank returns.

One day, Angus the Bank phoned me: 'Barrie, is that you?... Get off the line, this is private.'

There was a tell-tale 'click' as the operator disconnected herself.

'Are you there, Barrie? How are you? How're Marianne and the boys?' Without waiting for a reply, he ran on, 'Look, Barrie, I've received this quite indecent letter from Head Office about your overdraft. If it were up to me, I wouldn't worry at all. But we have to take notice of those unfeeling, unsympathetic lords and masters in Edinburgh. They are being very nasty indeed.'

My heart sank. I thought that Angus was leading up to the knock-out. How would I tell Marianne that we had reached the moment of truth, that we would have to sell?

He went on, 'In my view, they deserve little consideration, these beggars that live in the big city. They have no idea in the wur-rld of the tr-rials and tr-ribulations that haunt and persecute us here in these isolated areas with nothing but the sheep and the buzzards for company. Now look, Barrie... are you there? Good, I'll tell you what I'll do. I'll write you a very vicious letter – something to make your hair fr-rizzle on your head. But I won't ask you to read it because it will only upset you. I'll tear up the top copy and file the flimsy. Now remember, if the inspectors have occasion to call on you and ask if you've received this letter from me, tell them you know all about it! 'Bye, Barrie, and don't worry!'

He hung up. Somehow or other a Cheshire Cat grin had been transmitted down the line as he spoke; it was now floating in mid-air between me and the handset.

I walked over to where Marianne was sitting on the concrete floor of the theatre,

The
Mull Little
Theatre

"TWO BY TWO"

by Programme - 4/6

The
Mull Little
Theatre

presents
"THE TEMPEST"
by
WILLIAM SHAKESPEARE

Admission by Programme
8.30 p.m.

The
Mull Little
Theatre

presents
"MISS JULIE"
By August Strindberg
Translated from the Swedish by Elizabeth Sprigge

"THE BEAR"
By Anton Chekhov
Admission by Programme   4/6
8.30 p.m.

hemming the curtains. The big door was wide open, letting in the soft spring air. 'Angus the Bank just rang,' I said, 'and it doesn't take much reading between the lines to tell we're in trouble.' I related the conversation. I saw her face becoming set and her eyes gazing beyond mine. 'What shall we do?' she asked. 'Is the Bank going to foreclose?'

'Angus will hold off Head Office as long as possible,' I said.

'Can we stick it out for one more season?'

'Money will start coming in when the tourists arrive – not enough, but after all, this *is* the worst time of the year. We may just get by. And if we don't...' I shrugged, leaving the sentence unfinished.

'Well,' she looked towards the stage, 'if we've got to leave the island, we'll have done what we've always wanted to do and run a theatre, even if it was only for a few weeks.'

All this time, we felt that we had been standing on an ice floe about to break up under our feet. Nonetheless, we could see no way to improve our situation other than to stick with what we had decided to do.

We agreed to use as little outside help as possible to keep the wage bills down, and continue running the guesthouse. Drawing on our experience of weekly repertory theatre, we chose Thursday evenings as the best night for the shows and decided to charge four shillings and sixpence for a ticket. This, we hoped, would bring in an extra five or six pounds a week – not a sum to be sniffed at. If we managed to attract a few more people from the village to join the audience from the guesthouse that would be all to the good.

We were painfully aware that we were taking a big risk, so in order to give ourselves the best chance of success, we devoted our energies to devising and rehearsing a light-hearted programme of good quality material. This is what we came up with:

"TWO BY TWO"

Barrie and Marianne Hesketh present a light-hearted look at love and marriage

Part One

Mr and Mrs Noah	The Wakefield Play
O Western Wind	Traditional
A Prayer to St Catherine	Traditional
The Twa Corbies	Scots traditional
To Mistress Margaret Hussey	Skelton
Kate and Petruchio	The Taming of the Shrew
Come Live with Me	Marlowe
Pru and Tattle	Love for Love
Echo	Swift
The Scandal	Sternheim
Three Poems	D.H. Lawrence
A Railway Adventure	Molnár

Interval

Part Two
Village Wooing: a comedy by Bernard Shaw in three scenes

Scene 1 On board a pleasure ship
Scene 2 A village shop in Wiltshire
Scene 3 The same

Before we went to press with the programme, we had had to think about what the punters might like by way of refreshments during the interval, and what they would do if they wanted a pee. The second part was easy: the women could use the lavatories over in the main house and the men could nip round the back of the theatre, where there was a convenient copse of hazelnut trees.

'It would be nice,' said Marianne wistfully, remembering evenings at London theatres, 'to serve swish little chocolates and ice-creams.'

'Impossible,' I said.

'But we could do something nearly as good.' Marianne replied. 'I know a recipe for little chocolate cakes and, what's more, they're very easy to make.'[2]

Then, like so many other things in our lives, we realised we had started something which was to become quite an institution (and remained so until I finally left the Mull Little Theatre). As well as a being a traditional part of the Little Theatre experience, the cakes proved to be a good money-spinner. Eventually, we did not dare stop making them. Experience taught us that a full house of thirty-seven people could eat eighty of these cakes during the interval. But of course, by the time we had run for ten years, we ourselves really had had enough of them. By the twentieth year – and my last – I was delighted and relieved to think I would never ever have to make another. From the day we opened at Easter in 1966 to the day I left, I calculated that we had made – and our audience had consumed – about two hundred thousand of the beastly little things.

It was just as we were about to open the theatre for the first time that Angus the Bank phoned again.

'Barrie… get off the line… (click)… Barrie, your overdraft is causing great concern at Head Office. Now, you and I know perfectly well that everything is under control, but those in power at Head Office have no heart, no proper understanding of the way of the wur-rld here on Mull. To put it bluntly, you've no money at all and they are not happy about lending you any more. I'll tell what I'll do. I'll take out a life insurance in your name. Now, how much can you afford each week?'

---

2 The Mull Little Theatre Chocolate Cakes: 7 oz. melted margarine; 6 oz. plain flour; 3 oz. sugar; 2 oz. cornflakes; 1 oz. cocoa; 1/4 tsp. salt; 1 tsp. vanilla essence; chocolate glacé icing. Mix all the ingredients together and put spoonful of the mixture on a baking tray. Bake in a medium oven until firmly cooked, then top with chocolate icing.

'But Angus – you've just said I've no money.' 'That's quite right, not a penny! But a modest insurance will build up the necessary collateral that Head Office is looking for. Leave it all to me and don't worry; life's too short to worry over things like money. After all, the Bank's got plenty of it. Call in and see me when you're next in Tobermory. My love to Marianne…'

Notwithstanding the gathering clouds of doom and gloom, we painted a sign and put it at the bottom of the drive. It read: *1966 Season – Thursday Theatre. Curtain Up 8.30 p.m.*

Our guests were thrilled. But we ourselves suffered a bad attack of stage fright. Had we taken on more than we could manage? Could we look after the guests, perform in the theatre to a good standard *and* give love and time to the children? We were soon to find out.

'When you've finished your dinner,' we announced on that first evening, 'perhaps you would like to come over to the theatre. And…' because we hadn't quite finished fitting all the seating, 'please bring your dining chair with you.'

Our sons ran hither and thither, fetching and carrying. At last, everything was ready. Marianne, in a white blouse and long black skirt, positioned herself centre stage, clutching her Mrs Noah distaff. I, in black trousers and polo-neck sweater, stood by a decrepit record-player which was precariously balanced in the wings next to our curtain pull.

Opening night, 1966. Barrie and Marianne in the first scene of Village Wooing *by Bernard Shaw*

The auditorium light went out with a click; someone in the audience giggled. I cross-faded the 'coming in' music – Gershwin's jaunty *An American in Paris* – into the electrifying rhythms of *Le Sacré du Printemps* by Stravinsky. Marianne whispered, 'Thespis Aid Us' and then, to make double sure, 'Break a leg.' I faded out the music and, from behind the closed curtains, read the opening quotation we had chosen from Genesis.

Then, having quickly pulled back the curtains, we stepped on to our newly painted rostra – the inverted shop-counters – and began:

'Noah Godspeed, dear wife, how fare ye?

Wife Now, as ever might I thrive, the worse that I thee see…'

And once having begun, the end

came quickly. It was as though the whole performance had been a dream. Before we knew it, we were taking our bows. Then, from the stage, Marianne asked which of our guests would like evening tea and biscuits. We did a quick count and, still in costume and make-up, sped back to the kitchen. It was a cool night, so we put on plenty of hot water, both for bedtime tea and the guests' hot-water bottles.

The first night turned into a party that continued well into the early hours. Thereafter, however, with a guesthouse as well as a theatre to run, we made sure of conserving as much of our energy as possible.

Three weeks passed and, though tired, we were still going strong. Spurred on by the popularity of the show, we decided to put on two performances a week. I repainted

First season 1966. Kate and Petruchio

the sign at the bottom of the drive to read *Tuesday and Thursday Theatre*.

In those early days, we were lucky to know Zoe Middleton, who lived locally. She came to help sell tickets and see the audience into their seats. A table and chair were set up for her directly outside the big door. In fine weather, this was a job anyone would have enjoyed; but when it was stormy, it was a very different matter. Even under adverse circumstances, however, Zoe soon showed what stuff she was made of.

The only way into the auditorium was through the big door and when it opened there was nothing to stop the wind from whipping round the whole building and snatching at everyone's programmes. When it rained, heavy droplets found their way in, hitting the person closest to the door full in the face and drenching the laps of anyone else who happened to sit nearby. At such times, Zoe bravely stood outside in her anorak, collecting the money for the tickets. Then she would fetch the trays of chocolate cakes from the house, fifty feet away across the mud. This could be a hazardous passage if the wind was blowing hard; a sudden gust could quite easily carry off the cakes. Having transported them safely, Zoe would prepare for the interval, setting things up in the dressing-room backstage. She always managed to keep mousey quiet and never intruded on the action.

Towards the end of the first season, one of the house-guests staying with us, Major Sadler, introduced himself as a member of a charitable trust. Having explained about trusts and brought our attention to the advantages we might gain if our own theatre were to be registered as a charity, he asked if we wanted anything to help us expand our theatre work – anything, that was, on one special condition. This was that, no matter how worthy the trustees might deem our project to be, they could only consider applications from people with a Birmingham connection. I told him that by great good fortune I had been born in Erdington and that we badly needed a record-player. Hearing this, he became hopeful for us – even more so when I told him about my grandmother's 'good works'. I then showed him a photograph of Hesketh Crescent named after her, and he became entirely confident that we would get what we wanted.

We were given the record-player. Nevertheless, this one-off donation was hardly enough to reassure the bank that we would receive a regular input from charitable trusts from now on. Again, Angus called me: 'Barrie, is that you?… Get off the line, this is private … (click)… Barrie, how are you? Are you and Marianne and the children well? How are the guesthouse bookings?'

'Not very good…'

'No, no one is having an easy time, Barrie. But you're doing your best?'

'Yes, we are. Look, Angus – '

'I'll tell Head Office you're striving with might and main to make a go of it. In fact, I've nearly finished writing them a letter about your overdraft. It's a masterpiece of intricate nonsense. I'm determined to shut them up. I know you and Marianne are all right and will pull through, and I'm fed up with the High and Mighty trying to run this island as if they knew anything about it. They'll get this letter, full of the most arrant, well-written rubbish they've ever seen, and I doubt if we'll hear much from them again. 'Bye… my love to Marianne.'

Angus was the most astute banker in the west of Scotland. Apart from that, being bilingual, fluent in English and Gaelic, he was an ideal host at ceilidhs where he would recite his own light verses, some of which he published. He was a man of wit and imagination and there is no doubt at all that the Mull Little Theatre owed its start in life to him. He was a very good doctor to an extremely sickly baby.

By the end of our first summer season, it was obvious that we had made the right decision – indeed, that the theatre might be the saving of us. We now believed that another year would be feasible.

We had drawn a bow at a venture and the arrow had found its mark. What target were we to set ourselves next? We chose to adapt two short classic plays. The first would throw our audience into a mood of deep depression and the second, after the interval, would restore them with laughter.

8

Strangers in Paradise

The theatre now promised to be a success and this helped us feel that we stood a chance of a future on Mull. We began to look around the island and find out more about its history. At about this time, a new era was dawning: people began to visit the Hebrides in their thousands. This seems like an ironic reversal of what had happened a century before, when so many of the inhabitants had been forced to leave the land.

Before coming to Mull, neither Marianne nor I had known much about the Highland Clearances. Our first opportunity was when we were given John Prebble's book on the subject by someone who had lived on the island all his life. He thrust it into our hands with the words, 'If you're coming to live amongst us, read that; otherwise we will be strangers to one another.'

The Highlander has his roots buried deep in the past and will often tell tales of times long gone as if these events had taken place yesterday. This was brought home to me most poignantly when I was regaled with the story of a young couple, newly wed, who had been crushed to death beneath a rock that had slipped and flattened their little house. It was a horrific account and I felt greatly saddened. I later found out that the accident had happened over a hundred years ago; but it had been recounted as a contemporary tragedy. The pity it evoked in me had dissolved the passage of time and brought the past vitally into the present. The experience taught me a great deal about the power of the oral tradition, which proved to be something we were later to exploit in the Mull Little Theatre.[3]

Shortly after opening the theatre, we met Iain Crichton Smith, the poet and novelist. We were on tour and doing a performance at Oban High School, where Iain was then teaching in the English Department. After the show, he came and told us that the art of the theatre was virtually unknown to him, and that our production had inspired him to write for us. An honour indeed. However, since we knew that he came from the Island of Lewis and enjoyed a reputation as a writer in both Gaelic and English, we were very wary of taking on the responsibility of staging his work. We expected to get something that was wholly focused on life in the Highlands and Islands, and we worried about our ability to produce an authentic dialect. As it turned out, the theme of the first piece he wrote for us was the Cold War, and I had to purchase a record by the American monologist Ruth Draper, in order to master a variety of American accents. The drama revolves around the memories and dreams of an American president making the penultimate phone call to his counterpart in the Soviet Russia. It was a chilling piece called, quite simply, *Phones.*

3 Among recent publications on the history of the Highlands and Islands is *The Story of Mull and Iona*, written and illustrated by Nick Hesketh

Marianne with the 'robot' shadow puppet from Iain Crichton Smith's Waiting for the Train

Over the years, Iain wrote many short plays for us. Several were inspired by Shakespeare's *Hamlet*. I remember one, in particular, that was set in a Chinese restaurant in Oban, where a middle-aged Ophelia and Hamlet were in conversation over a bowl of chop suey – until they felt compelled to leave as King Claudio and Queen Gertrude made an appearance. Iain's imagination ranges far and wide, drawing on ideas from Kierkegaard to Borges, Buster Keaton to Agatha Christie.

It was some time before we received a play from him written about the Highlands. Called *A Kind of Play*, his two characters take the audience into an intricate comedy, where the downfall of Prince Charlie is perceived through the eyes of a budding playwright who owes much to the effects of love, whisky and detective story writing. It is both very sad and very funny. Although set in a local Highland context, it contains the universal message: 'Lord, what fools these mortals be'. For me, as a performer, it has much of the power and appeal of Chekhov's short works for the theatre.

Many Highlanders emigrated, sometimes naming their new homes after the ones they had left behind. For a time, I thought Calgary, in Canada, was one of these nostalgic names. The area known as Calgary on the north west coast of Mull contains a stunningly beautiful beach. It is set within an amphitheatre of heavily-wooded, flat-topped hills and, as they curve down towards the sea like enfolding arms, they stand stark – the sinews of old lava flows showing through the thin skin of grasses. Under the northern arm runs a rutted cart track to a granite pier that, in the setting sun, glows a soft pink. The sand – almost pure white – shelves very gently and children are safe there. On the landward side, just across a narrow, dusty white road are fields of cattle and woods surrounding the fine Calgary House. Even in the stormiest weather, I have always thought of Calgary Bay as possessing a mysterious air of tranquillity.

In the midst of this peace there is a very old burial ground. There are a few graves and these lie next to the grass-covered remains of a small chapel. All is watched over by a protective screen of elegant trees. It is here in this sacred grove that the *genius loci* resides.

It turned out that I was wrong to assume the Calgary in Canada to have been a clearance name. Instead, the story as it was told me goes as follows. In 1875, Macleod, an officer with the North West Mounted Police, was negotiating a site for a new fort. His opposite number was the man who had seen General Custer off the map at the battle of Little Big Horn: Big Chief Sitting Bull, an Indian of stubborn mind, not easily convinced by the arguments put forward by the British officer. Their discussion had reached an impasse – there seemed to be no way of coming to an agreement. Then, all of a sudden, the Chief noticed Macleod's signet ring. He asked if he might look at it more carefully; from then on, the negotiations proceeded smoothly.

Apparently, what had eased the transaction was the sight of Macleod's crest – a bull! The two men shared the same totem and were consequently brothers. Macleod was so pleased with himself for having brought the matter to a successful outcome that he was all for naming the fort after himself. His fellow officers, however, persuaded him that this would not be appropriate. Instead, therefore, having recently returned from a pleasant holiday with the Mackenzies of Calgary, he named it after the venue.

There is an old Highland saying that 'news improves with the telling' and this exemplifies it well. Later on, I came to doubt the authenticity of the first account when I discovered that there was in fact a Fort Macleod – named after Col. James F. Macleod – which, like Calgary, was also in Alberta. It would appear that, somewhere along the line, the tale had been tampered with. Nevertheless, after a long time of living on a Scottish island, I have come to value the embellishments that accrue from story-telling as a valid part of the historical process; it is those subtle additions and modifications which reflect the person's wish to tell you what he or she thinks you want to know. Tales such as the one about Macleod do not necessarily convey material fact but, rather, the special personal relationship between the teller and the listener.

The Highland preoccupation with the past strikes me as indicative of the fact that dealings between the clans and the government were rarely satisfactory. Without an intimate knowledge of either Scottish mainland or Highland history, the habit of harking back to the distant past can be bewildering.

The postmistress in Dervaig, like many of the Gaelic speakers on the island, had come to live on Mull from one of the other islands. One day shortly after our arrival, I was in the Post Office waiting to be served. The postmistress and old Kate were chatting in Gaelic and there came a point when, with a little smile in my direction, the postmistress said the word 'sassenach' – meaning a stranger from the south.

After Kate had left the shop, she asked, 'Do you mind being called a sassenach, Barrie?'

'Not at all; that's what I am.'

'Well,' she went on, looking me straight in the eye, 'I'd rather be called a sassenach than a Campbell!' Being a sassenach, with none of the old partisanship that runs through Gaeldom, I responded somewhat lamely. Then, feeling rather at a loss, I continued, 'Could I have a pound of carrots, please?' Stamps were not the only thing on sale at the Post Office.

I've often wondered if she was trying to find out from me, a comparative newcomer

Mull Little Theatre and the view west

to the village, whether I was affiliated to Us, the Gaels in general, or Them, the Campbells. This would have been a matter of some importance.

The searing effects of the Clearances seem to have inclined the Highlander to think better of the English than of the Lowland Scots. The argument behind this can be summed up thus: the English landlords were 'just plain ignorant,' whereas the Scots should have understood and therefore had more sympathy for the plight of their countrymen. I knew a Highland television mechanic who, for this reason, refused to buy his electronic supplies from Scotland, believing that he got better service south of the border.

Nowadays, the island is made up of a very mixed community. At one time it was known locally as 'the Officers' Mess'. During their stint in the armed forces, majors and captains had dreamt of retiring to a quiet country life and had bought property there. However, as many others have also found, Mull was more alluring than fulfilling. I heard of several officers who tried to let out land for shooting; others who had set up poultry farms; and even one or two who attempted to breed mink. But the mink escaped and, by making themselves a nuisance to the poultry farmers, at least gave the hunters something to shoot at. Many people have been attracted to this inviting island, only to have their dreams shown up for what they were – mere dreams. After that first thrill, they have given up and left, sadder and wiser. I don't know if there is any single attribute that makes it possible to stay the course, but anyone who lives on the island for long will, sooner or later, come face to face with themselves. It is this that sometimes proves too much of a challenge.

We, too, would have gone the way of the disappointed had we not been, as it were, 'on the game'. There is an element of whoring in acting; we offer ourselves for money and, no matter how we are feeling, the public may use our bodies, our voices, our person-alities to feed their imaginations, night after night. Like prostitutes (and, to a certain extent, the island itself), we allowed people to project their dreams on to us. At every performance we emptied a part of our being in order to become a receptacle for other people's fantasies. At the risk of losing touch with common humanity, we had to accept the ineluctable process of this mythologising. Because we were not always what we seemed, we could never wholly become an integral part of the community.

Early days of the Mull Little Theatre: the audience arriving

9

Northern Lights

We were now in our mid-thirties and at the height of our energy. I cannot conceive how, at any other age, we could have successfully juggled the three major elements in our lives – running the theatre, managing the guesthouse and bringing up our family.

The boys, for their part, were now completely accustomed to the countryside: the woods and hills, the shallow loch and the overgrown garden were all their playground. We did not have to worry unduly about where they were or what they were doing – it was a challenging but safe world for them. During the theatre season, when they were still quite small and had been put to bed in the hut, we would read to them before going over for the performance. Each night we impressed upon them that, though we were actors, we were their parents first and that in any emergency they must not hesitate in coming over to the theatre and asking for us.

In fact, they never did. On the contrary, the boys took advantage of our absence. They would climb out of the bedroom windows dressed in their pyjamas and wellington boots, and play on the flower-covered hill behind the house. It was always part of any game they had invented to move away from the hut as far as they dared, yet remain sufficiently close to the theatre to hear the applause which announced an interval. Then they would run as fast as they could, scramble back into the hut through the windows – the door was open, but through the windows it had to be – and be snuggled down and breathing evenly, pretending to be asleep before either Marianne or I found time between the acts to see whether they were all right or if they wanted anything.

On fine evenings, they would hold court and, leaning out of their windows, wave and chat to members of the audience as they crossed from the car park to the theatre. I can see them now – keeping Paul and Joy Scofield in conversation on their occasional visits to the theatre. Three little heads: one blue-eyed and mousy-haired – Richard; one brown-eyed and brown-haired – Nicholas; and one very fair-haired with green eyes – Jim; Joy stands close, petite and pretty, and Paul towers over them all, his mellifluous voice carried on the light summer air penetrating our dressing room.

It was not long after we had started the theatre that the questions began: 'Why Mull?' and 'What do you do in the winter?' As for the latter, this could be fobbed off with 'We hibernate,' or some such joke; but 'Why Mull?' was more difficult to answer. People really wanted to know, especially as the quality of our theatre work was of a high standard. We would say we had come because we wanted to bring up the children in a rural environment; that Marianne had wanted to write and I had wanted to paint; and that theatre on the mainland had taken rather a severe knock from the success of television. This kind of answer received sympathetic nods.

What we did not admit was our irrational fear of the Bomb; this had been a very

Richard, aged 11, handing round the cakes

powerful element in our motivation to come to the island. It was in the interests of our business to gloss over and make beautiful the whole of the Mull experience. Romanticism was all! If we ever let the darker side show – irritation with living condi-tions, for example – it was met with disbelief, sometimes outright denial. People did not want us to take off the mask, especially not while they were on holiday.

In 1968, we undertook our first really ambitious production, one that was to prove we could run as well as walk: Shakespeare's *The Tempest*.

Here, I am reminded of Donald MacKechnie, a local character who would have delighted Shakespeare. It was his job to go round the Dervaig area with a spade and dig round the drains, to see that they were in good order. He came to all our shows. Of *The Tempest* he said, 'What a pity the man didn't write in the Gaelic!'

He himself was a great spinner of tales, never telling anyone what they didn't want to hear. He would keep our sons amused at the crossroads while they waited for the school-bus in the mornings, regaling them with entertaining but highly unlikely stories. He once told two girl hikers who had asked him the way to the theatre that when they found it, it would 'look like a wee byre'. Then he went on: 'But don't be put off, because what you see is actually the front porch of a building built into the hill. And once you're inside, you'll be flabbergasted by the immensity of it, for the cave goes on and on. In fact, you'll find that it's bigger than La Scala in Milan – and all under the hill – imagine that!'

The girls were all keyed-up for a grand experience. The let-down made them so giggly during the performance that they apologised to us for making a nuisance of themselves which, as we were playing a comedy that night, they certainly hadn't.

'I'm coming up to the Ceilidh tonight,' Donald would tell me and, in answer to my query, he told me what a real ceilidh had been like in the old days. It could have been quite a small affair, he explained, with people coming together to have 'a crack' over a cup of tea or a whisky. There used to be what was known as the 'ceilidh house' in most Highland villages, which was a meeting place, a sort of village parliament. All the villagers would gather together, each person contributing something to the evening. If there were any arguments, they would be settled; children would tell stories or ask conundrums. There would be a dance, of course, and the fiddler would fiddle and the piper would pipe. 'And if there was anybody there like you, Barrie – come in from the outside world,' said Donald, ' well, you'd be invited to tell of your adventures.' But that sort of thing has died out. Ceilidhs are now nothing more than village concerts.

I learnt a valuable lesson from the modern ceilidh. This was that you can be very informal and friendly with your audience up until the performance begins; but thereafter you are as professional as you can possibly be. I adapted this Highland practice to our own theatre. I would come out in front of the curtains prior to the start of the show, talk to the audience as myself – a human being, not an actor wearing a mask – and tell them how the day had gone for us, perhaps including a story about the boys, just to make it more personal. I did that every night, every show, including the shows on tour. There were times when I'd think to myself how boring and twee this must sound! Occasionally, introducing ourselves in this way became so tedious that I asked if I should stop. We discovered that it was only our academic friends who were turned off by it – perhaps because an actor's charm is anathema to the Higher and Rarefied Mind. But everyone else seemed to like it, so it remained a regular feature to the very end.

We did once hold a 'proper' ceilidh for everyone from the mainland who had done so much to encourage us develop the theatre. Amongst the guests were Winnie Ewing, then a Scottish Nationalist MP, and Robert Ponsonby, one-time Director of the Edinburgh Festival.

The party was held over a weekend in winter. The weather was calm but cold; the aurora borealis lit up the night sky with fantastic flares that, in the blink of an eye, would switch from flickering searchlights to wavering, luminous cobwebs which spread for thousands of miles. Once, an iridescent eagle hovered over the house, its strange, shimmering wings stretching from horizon to horizon. It must have been the craggy eagle of Crianlarich in flight! Or even that eagle we'd seen in the tea-leaves on our honeymoon. We took this to be a very happy sign for the future. The party went wonderfully well, and the boys helped by feeding enormous log fires with wood gathered from fallen trees in the garden.

These fires had certainly warmed us, but they had also heated up a timber beam behind the bathroom wall, situated directly above the living room. Two days later, after all the guests had gone home, Nicholas, then aged about ten, was enjoying his nightly bath. He looked up from soaping himself and saw a little flash of flame glinting from a small gap between the window-frame and the wall. With great presence of mind, he got out of the bath and put on his dressing-gown and slippers. Then, still dripping, he walked steadily and slowly down the stairs to the living room where Marianne, Richard and myself were sitting reading. Jim, already in bed, was surrounded by books and oblivious to the world.

'Excuse me, fire,' he whispered.

'What did you say, Nick?' asked Marianne.

'Fire.' The word was quite clearly enunciated but still whispered.

'Fire?' we enquired, wondering whether we had heard correctly.

'Where is the fire, dear?' We couldn't believe our ears.

Again, whispered and precisely articulated, 'Fire! In the bathroom!'

At last, the seriousness of what he was saying got through to us.

'FIRE!' we all shouted.

Much later, Nicholas explained how he had had impressed upon him the importance of not spreading panic in the event of an emergency in the theatre. This had been the thought uppermost in his mind as he had come downstairs and told us the news.

As a device to keep the populace calm, this was obviously very effective. In this case, however, once we'd got the message, we moved fast. 'Show me!' I yelled, chasing after Nick who had turned on his heels and was running back upstairs. He pointed. I applied my eye to the crack. No doubt about it – there was fire! Although small, it was extremely fierce, burning white hot as it consumed the resin from the logs adhering to the wood and stone of the wall.

One of the horrors of fire on Mull was the time it could take for help to arrive. Distances and single-track roads, sometimes blocked by herds of cattle, created frightening problems.

I didn't think there was any immediate danger, so Richard and I went out to get a ladder and look for a length of hose that I was sure to find somewhere in the garden. We fetched the ladder and ran upstairs with it back to the bathroom. We leant it against the trap-door leading to the loft. There, with the boys close behind me, I heaved myself up into the roof and scrambled quickly over the joists to a position where I could look down the narrow gap running between the outside wall and the inside lath and plaster. The fire was healthy, but as yet concentrated in only one spot. Marianne passed me a bucket of water; I slipped and spilt most of it over her and the children. I tried to aim what was left into the wall cavity – with no success. The fire continued to spit and glow ominously.

'We *must* find the hose. Come on, Richard!'

We returned to the garden. The torch was too dim to be of any use and I knew we had no replacement batteries; I was beginning to feel a tight knot of fear developing in my stomach. It would take at least half-an-hour for the Fire Service to get to us. Was fire, again, going to end a dream?

The hose could not be found (although the following morning I saw it tied to a branch, high up a tree). I ran back into the house to phone for help. Just as I was picking up the receiver, there were excited shouts from Marianne and Jim. 'It's out. Panic over!'

'How do you mean, it's out?' I asked.

'Nick spat it out.'

'He what?' Then, very breathlessly and trying not to show his pride, Nick told us what he'd done. He had filled his mouth with bath water, put his lips against the cranny in the wall and directed a stream of soapy water towards the flames. By repeating this over and over again, with commendable determination and accuracy, he had indeed put out the fire. I went up into the loft to check. There was no tell-tale glow.

Then, quite without warning, Nick began to shake. We took him to bed, suffering from delayed shock.

From then on, we took care to have sufficient fire-fighting equipment to hand, including a torch that always worked.

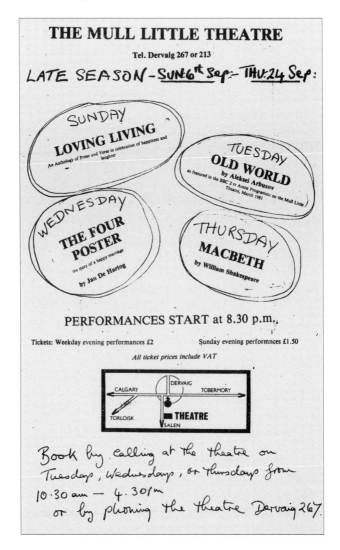

10

Players' Work Time

The nature of our work isolated us from the community, even though the community was very willing to reach out towards us and be friendly. We had chosen to stand slightly aside so as to maintain an objectivity that – rightly or wrongly – we believed was necessary to the craft of acting and the art of theatre. And watching from the side-lines, notwithstanding the island's mixed demography – or perhaps because of it – we thought we noticed a strain of feudalism. Although undoubtedly on the wane, this was still recognisable in the relationship that existed between them-as-have and them-as-have-not.

We looked for a play that reflected such differences of class but which would, at the same time, suit our audiences. We lighted on Elizabeth Sprigge's translation of Strindberg's *Miss Julie*. Since we realised that rehearsals for this play were likely to be fraught with anguish, we decided to play Chekhov's farce, *The Bear*, in tandem with the Strindberg. The two proved to be a fine complement for each other.

The fury and passion which blossom in Chekhov's protagonists gave us a much-needed release from the tension created between the characters in *Miss Julie*.[4] It was not difficult for us to identify with the intense frustration – and its tragic effects – portrayed by Strindberg. But just as importantly, *The Bear* allowed us to give vent to feelings which we shared with Smirnov, the Bear of the title, who had also lived under threat of financial failure.

It is par for the course that there are moments during rehearsal when tempers flare and nerves fray. Clashes of personality or differences of interpretation can bring on fine shows of temperament; few rehearsals of the plays we presented were without these flash points. In the case of *Miss Julie*, although Marianne and I were in harmony with each other, for much of the rehearsal time we felt distinctly out of tune with the play and its author. How we solved our problems with August Strindberg remains sharply engraved on my memory.

Miss Julie is an 'Upstairs, Downstairs' drama. Jan, a butler, aspires to leave his life of service in the big house to become his own master, owning and managing a hotel. One midsummer night, he sees an opportunity to realise his dreams of escaping the feudal tyranny by responding to the sexual taunts of the daughter of the house. He forces her to submit to him. Things go badly wrong and the play finishes with Julie, apparently acting on Jan's instructions, leaving his presence to put an end to her life somewhere off-stage.

---

4 Both *Miss Julie* and *The Bear* have casts of three, but Marianne had adapted the plays so that they could be played as two-handers

We had always admired Strindberg's work as being psychologically accurate. At first, the rehearsals went well. But eventually we reached a point when neither of us could say the lines that led to Julie's supposed final exit. It was as though a heavy gate slammed shut in front of us when we got to the part where she takes the decision to end it all. Everything we did or said sounded wrong; the tenor of the play shifted from tragedy to melodrama and we were not prepared to cross the fine line dividing the one from the other.

What was wrong? We talked it through, we acted it through, again and again, only to be met with the same slam of the gate. We drank coffee by the jugful; we improvised moves and tried out innumerable intonations and inflections; we looked at each other in disbelief. We were unable to find the motivation to carry the play forward to the end. Finally, we both gave up and burst into tears – the tears of manifold bafflement. Julie's elusive character had become identified with what we felt towards our life in general. So much so, that it was always a relief when the boys came home from school in the afternoon; we could then break the rehearsal and forget Julie and Jan. However, with the boys back at school the next morning, we were again having to face 'that intractable bitch', as Marianne called her.

'Strindberg has made a mistake. There's no logic in it!' Marianne was in despair over the part. I, too, felt at a loss. There was nothing I could do in the character of Jan to further the action. How could we perform a piece, written by an author we admired a great deal, but which was now proving so soul-destroying?

There was no going back. Time was beginning to press upon us. We couldn't simply jettison *Miss Julie*, look for another play and begin all over again. Once it was in the repertoire, we had no alternative but to continue with it until the end of the season. It was imperative to get it right from the start.

'I can't do it,' Marianne said. 'She does not commit suicide as the script suggests.' Hindsight tells me that this affirmation of life, an unusual interpretation of the part of Julie, was indeed the result of intellectual honesty, but also of Marianne's own desperation. There was a shadow hovering near her – a tendency to give a sympathetic hearing to the whisperings of suicide, but which she had always fought against.

She became angry. 'She'll pick up Jan's razor; but she does not follow through, of that I am convinced. Not in a million years would she cut her throat. And I mustn't leave the audience in any doubt about this.'

Harking back to the days when we held hands in the Classic Cinema in the King's Road, and hoping that thinking of the play in different terms might help solve the problem, I asked her to imagine that she was making a film. 'Julie walks along the bank of a river,' Marianne began. 'Mist and reeds and early morning birdsong. There is a close-up shot of her eyes; they are confused, but petulant rather than despairing. Then she makes as if to slash her wrists. She'd give in to hysterics well within earshot of the people at the big house; her cries are meant to be heard. Lots of remorse. But she does not die. Strindberg's women do not die that easily!'

Marianne looked up. 'How the hell am I to show all that?' As she asked the question, she found the answer. With one simple gesture, she would display Julie's infirmity of purpose as she made her final exit. We were back on track and the play recovered its dignity.

We were to receive two confirmations that Marianne had interpreted the character correctly. We read later that, in the first performance, Strindberg had had Julie cutting her wrists on stage. However, there had been complaints from his audience. He therefore re-wrote the scene, merely suggesting that she is about to take her own life in earnest – off-stage.

The other confirmation came from a friend, Dr Jimmy Macdougall, a psychiatrist who worked at the Argyll and Bute Hospital. After seeing our performance, we discussed Marianne's reluctance to accept the usual view. Taking a large pinch of snuff, he pointed out dryly that, 'As a rule of thumb, a lassie who has just been well and truly laid, in the manner Marianne portrays her, does not go and cut her throat. She might cry for help later, when the going gets tough – and that indeed might take the form of cutting her wrists – but no, no, no, I wouldn't expect her to cut her throat.'

He advocated the showing of *Miss Julie* throughout the length and breadth of Argyll: 'As I see it,' he said, 'the play gets at the truth of much of what's wrong in this part of the country.'

When we performed *Miss Julie* one evening before an audience entirely made up of two large households – the lairds and their wives had brought their complete retinue of cooks and servants – the divisions between upstairs and downstairs were palpable: they invaded the stage. In the audience, loyalties became clear as soon as the theme of the play was revealed.

Elizabeth Sprigge, the translator, made the journey to Mull to see us in action. We were very nervous about having her in the audience; however, she not only signed our copy of her book, *Twelve Plays by Strindberg*, 'in admiration and affection', but also waived royalties on any work of hers we chose to use in future.[5]

Following Strindberg's dark drama, we had wanted to reflect all that was magical, amusing and life-enhancing about Mull. That was why we adapted *The Tempest*, Shakespeare's great pantomimic play, for just the two of us plus three life-size puppets. This quaint production attracted a lot of attention and publicity and strengthened our resolve to concentrate on the theatrical side of our endeavours.

One of the many spin-offs was that it encouraged us to scale down plays with large casts to suit our straightened circumstances. Amongst these was another play by Strindberg, *The Bond*, in which we took the part of a couple in a divorce case. The other members of the cast we recorded. The sound was fed into the auditorium through several loudspeakers rescued from defunct radios and the old record-player.

This production was so successful that later, when the Scottish Arts Council granted the Mull Little Theatre a considerable sum of money to replace our own inadequate machinery with excellent professional equipment, we were able to present a world première of Chekhov's *Tatyana Repin*. This production used ten powerful loudspeakers placed strategically around the inside of the theatre to create a play for sound

5 *The Bond, The Stronger*, and *The Great Highway*

The audience seen from the stage, with Marianne in profile

only. Marianne and I, by doing awful things to our throats, managed to find enough voices between us to create the cast of over thirty. Again, I was impressed by the importance of the oral tradition in the Hebrides. Several local people revisited the theatre to experience this production more than once. They commented on how real it had seemed to them. There were, of course, other members of the audience who were nonplussed by the lack of visual clues.

The other play that we adapted in this way was Bernard Shaw's *St Joan*, and we gave our first performance between the church services one Sunday in August in Iona Abbey.

Back in the Little Theatre, our inventiveness in adapting the classics to suit its tiny stage had just caught the attention of a small but prestigious college in the United States – Earlham, Indiana. Biannually, a group of students together with their tutors came from Indiana to study Scotland, both the country and its people. As part of their curriculum, the Professor of English had arranged to bring some of the students over to Mull for weekend teach-ins with us; in fact, this was exactly how we had always hoped the guesthouse might be used, specifically as a service to the theatre.

At this time, the draft for the war in Vietnam was in operation and, since the College was a Quaker foundation, a lot of soul-searching was going on amongst the young men. The young women were worried about what their brothers and boyfriends would do when they were called up.

On one particular visit, the students could be found sitting disconsolately on the hill behind the house, contemplating the risks facing them were they to tear up their draft

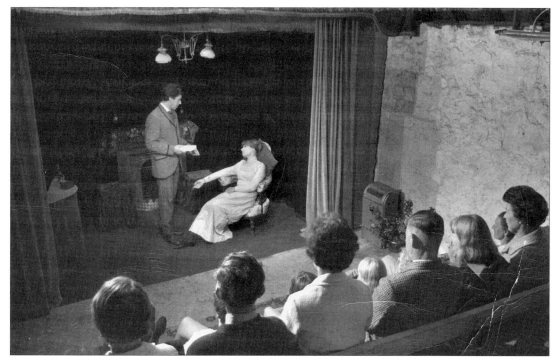

The Mull Little Theatre stage from the auditorium.
Barrie and Marianne in Jules Renard's Daily Bread

cards in protest. The same weekend, we also happened to have the artist, Mark Boyle, camping in our garden in an old ambulance he had converted into a dormobile. Having just begun to make an international reputation for himself, Mark was spending some time with his family on Mull in order to make one of his special pictures of part of Calgary.

At first, the students politely ignored him. Then, the news got round that Mark had been very close to Jimi Hendrix, with whom he had worked until shortly before Hendrix's death. This information brought about a miraculous change: the students could now be found sitting at Mark's feet, listening to him talking about 'the Master'. It was a myth in creation.

By now, we had the anthology *Two by Two*, *Miss Julie*, *The Bear*, *The Tempest* and *St Joan* in repertoire and we found that the amount of office work was growing in leaps and bounds. We had the guesthouse enquiries to answer, but we also began to look towards the idea of creating small tours of our theatre work. This meant sending out information about our productions and, in return, receiving brochures and bookings from arts centres and theatres all over the country.

It was then that a Scottish solicitor visited the guesthouse and stayed on to enjoy a show. On his return to the mainland, he did us a very good turn by bringing our name to the attention of a colleague, John Boyle (Mark's brother), who was on the Board of the Scottish Arts Council. Great good was to come of this informal connection between them – even though it struck us as unfair that our own local solicitor, who had been so kind and supportive to us when we came to the island, should have been lumbered with the horrific task of setting up the theatre as a limited company. By the time he had finished with the intricacies of company law – not, I should imagine, an issue often encountered in a small Highland village – I am sure he must have been teetering on the brink of nervous collapse.

Nevertheless, on March 29 1968, the Dervaig Arts Theatre Company was founded and duly registered as a charity. It was essential for the future health of the Little Theatre that this step be taken. It meant that the Theatre Company could now legitimately receive support from the Scottish Arts Council and other similar grant-aiding bodies.

To top up the grants and what we made at the box office, we came to rely on donations from our generous, long-suffering friends; from passers-by who dropped cash into our money box; and from money raised during the interval selling coffee, chocolate cakes and copies of *The Druimard Cook Book*, a collection of recipes Marianne and I had compiled. We pulled in our belts ever tighter.

In 1969, we were afforded marvellous relief. The Michael Marks Charitable Trust sent a grant which enabled us to build a foyer, buy a van for touring and employ a stage manager. Marianne suggested that I do a few paintings to brighten up the bare walls of the new foyer. We had not intended to put the paintings up for sale; but as fast as I hung them, people wanted to buy them. My oils were too 'strange' to attract buyers on Mull; on the other hand, the watercolours were executed in traditional style and they sold as rapidly as I could paint them. So rapidly, in fact, that – in between running the theatre, as well as making the cakes, overseeing our small number of staff and helping to bring up the children – I spent whatever time there was left painting.

The Mull Little Theatre's financial transactions with the Scottish Arts Council had begun under the guiding hand of John Faulkner, the then Drama Director. He had first come to Mull on a fact-finding mission. Then, with a briefcase full of figures about our finances, he had stayed on to see a show.

From time to time, Dervaig village and the surrounding farms were cut off from the electricity supply, usually because of a fault on the mainland. We lost power the night John was in the audience but were not long in providing alternative illumination. We lit a Tilley lamp and hung it near the exit; another went into the dressing-room and candles provided light in the lavatories. Having seen to the essentials, we gave John two powerful torches to hold, one in each hand, to be used as follow-spots on Marianne and me as we continued with the action of the play. He sat on the window-sill at the side of the audience and, with the unerring sense of timing of a one-time touring technician, switched them off pat on cue as Marianne said the tag line. I like to think that John's impeccable flair for artistry learned with the Prospect Theatre Company pleased the demon of drama that night. He was to become Head of Artistic Planning at the National Theatre.

Without charitable status, the Little Theatre would most likely have failed by the next year at the latest, and quickly been lost to memory. We had been advised not to call it the Mull Little Theatre Company – I cannot remember why, because it was always known as that. However, I do know why it was suggested that we get a 'big name' as a founder member of the Company: it was so as to get us good publicity. We wrote to several friends in the hope that one of them might be happy to be associated with a tiny theatre trust in the Hebrides. Not one replied – they all did! To our delight, we gained the support of some very influential people, amongst them the late Jeremy Brett and Robert Stephens; Harold Pinter, Robert Ponsonby and Paul Scofield.

Our publicity, at least at the launch of the Company, was assured. We could now apply for public money. Over the years, we found this a heartbreaking and time-consuming job; neither of us felt competent to handle the enormous postbag that developed as we approached more and more people. Nor were we really cut out for begging for money – though when it arrived, it was always very welcome.

Marianne would later stub her toes on the ethical questions concerning applications to any trusts which also had an interest in giving to health organisations. She always thought of health as a top priority. A doctor of our acquaintance told us not to be silly, firmly pronouncing his belief that the arts were of more importance to the health of mankind than aseptic surgery. I was encouraged by this view, stated in so positive a manner. However, Marianne remained unconvinced, perhaps because the future was already casting a shadow over her.

Raising money requires a special kind of aptitude and we found that we had to harden our hearts and become keenly acquisitive. It had always seemed to me that artists have their feet hovering an inch or two above the ground, whereas businessmen have theirs

Barrie at the door of the new foyer

firmly planted in the muck, where the brass is. We developed a kind of spiritual limp, hobbling with one foot on and the other foot off the ground. The hours we spent preparing documents to urge trusts to support us became a serious irritant. What is more, it was obvious to us that these cap-in-hand exercises were seriously undermining the work we were trying to sell. We were never free of this dilemma. We either had to use up valuable time raising money and risk lowering our standard of work; or concentrate on improving the quality of work and face the possibility of closure through lack of funds. Our company was never large enough to employ a business manager. It was also problematic that, as employees of the Company, Marianne and I could not sit on the Board.

However, the Scottish Arts Council was prepared to support us – on one condition, which was that we agree to tour during the winter months. We knew that if we accepted their terms, there would be little time left to prepare worthwhile productions. Neither would these winter tours be a simple matter of trotting round the Islands; they would inevitably involve long treks into the wildest parts of Scotland, England and Wales.

Ultimately, we had no choice. Frustrating though it was, we cancelled our plans to produce Sophocles' *Ajax* and decided to divert our energies into the duller, but necessary task of theatre management.

11

Swapping Hats, Changing Masks

The post used to be delivered to us in the late afternoon, sometimes after sunset. There were often up to twenty letters to deal with, and this could severely disrupt family life, especially during the winter season. The boys grew to hate the constant clacking of the typewriter.

Nevertheless, for Richard, that meant an evening walk with me to the post-box in the village – something he looked forward to because there was always so much to hear and see. Without the artificial glow of street lamps, the night was freer to express itself in its own way. There were the mysterious 'clops' in the river, the primeval 'crawks' from the herons, the squeaking of mice and the shrieking of owls. Sharp points of starlight were reflected, torn up and scattered in the little rills that ran beside the road. We would try and identify the trees by their blue-black silhouettes. Occasionally, it was possible to sight the two planets that seemed to influence our lives on Mull: the brilliant blue of Venus, offering love; and the bellicose red of Mars, bringer of conflict, confusion and the threat of banishment.

Richard and I would get home again in time for the last part of a night-time story with Nick and Jim. Then, after all the children had gone to bed, Marianne and I, with the cat sitting between us, would listen to our records. An idyllic domestic scene.

Living on Mull without street lighting made me more aware than ever before of the essential importance of festivals celebrating light. It wasn't just the children who looked forward to Christmas. We all anticipated with real pleasure the moment when the seven-foot evergreen was brought into the house, set up in a bucket of earth in a corner of the living room and decorated like some froward pagan bride, her gaudy skirts swelling out with the promise of a New Year birth.

The hundreds of cards we received from supporters of the Little Theatre – a surprising number of whom had become personal friends – also helped to expel the darkness. The dead of winter being a time when our enthusiasm for working in an isolated area was at its lowest, messages from admired colleagues at the top of our profession always gave us an extra fillip. So whenever Bernard Miles, Michael Redgrave or Richard Briers gave a wave of the flag, our morale soared.

And of course, while Marianne and I were riding the swings and roundabouts, the boys put up with us. They managed magnificently: besides enriching our lives, they added greatly to the ease of running the whole venture. Being brought up in the milieu of the theatre – and in a Highland context – they received an idiosyncratic education. Formal teaching, especially what they were offered at the local high school in Oban, had tended to run off them like water off a duck's back. During the week, they had to stay in the school hostel or live in digs. This proved an altogether unsatisfactory expe-

Scene from Jan de Hartog's The Four Poster

rience and they were always eager to come back to us at the weekends.

Marianne did not think of herself as a clinger. However, when our sons were at home, she found herself trapped in the age-old conflict. There was the appeal of caring and catering for them alongside the lure of the theatre not fifty feet from the kitchen – pull devil, pull baker. She hoped they would never be tempted to feel guilty about leaving her, as she so obviously enjoyed her devil's work and was happy to be left to get on with it. Nevertheless, she was in for a surprise at the strength of her reaction the first time they left home for school on the mainland – and when they eventually flew the nest.

It was at times like these that being in touch with the local community was a steadying influence. This, in turn, affected our attitude to the theatre. For example, the hectic business of doing everything ourselves because we lived on an island and in the country, put a stop to any pretensions we might have had about 'preparing our minds' before performing (in the good old theatrical tradition). A sheep farmer doesn't 'prepare his mind' before going out on the hill; he laces up his boots – his 'heather-lopers' – and gets on with it. Similarly, we became very down to earth about what we did. We would rush on stage, shout out the lines, get off and pray that what we'd done had been acceptable, before moving on to the next pressing item on our agenda, be it selling coffee in the foyer, taking the temperature of an ailing child or writing to a trust.

Notwithstanding the concreteness of family life, of keeping the Little Theatre open and the Company solvent, we did not escape being romanticised. And even in the small

Scene from Arbuzov's Old World, *Hildesheim*

doses we received, it was heady stuff and quite dangerous.

To the public – and to quite a number of our friends – Barrie and Marianne Hesketh were no longer individuals, nor the parents of a family *per se*. We belonged to the public dream machine. The late David James MP nicknamed us the 'Bariannes', echoing seaside concert parties and a period long gone. For many others, we were just 'the Little Theatre people' or 'the couple on *Late Night Line-up*'. We were sometimes identified by having been spotted in this or that magazine. It was a strange experience to be sent an article describing us in words we did not understand – Japanese, Polish, Finnish or Portuguese; we then became foreigners to ourselves. But of course, since we were always a little unsure of our identities anyway, we found ourselves searching the media unwittingly for clues.

Added to this, we began to realise that we had absorbed various aspects of the dramatic characters we knew well. Lines would pop into our heads unbidden, no longer as formal quotations, but as integral parts of Barrie and Marianne. If we were having a heated argument, we were never alone. Someone else, a character from one of the plays in our repertoire, would enter in and contribute a phrase here, a gesture there. We were used to life informing art, but to meet an example of the converse in a moment of anger was instructive.

Like every actor who has ever lived, we also had to contend with being seen, not as ourselves, but as the characters we played. Audiences project their fantasies on to actors. To escape the pernicious result of this 'transference', actors tend to don a special mask after removing the one used during performance. Paradoxically, there may be occasions when an actor does not wear a mask on stage, but then puts one on to meet his or her public. This serves as a shield from too much reflection of the audience's dreams; it also saves the actor from nakedness. Immediately after a performance, we actors are raw, sensitive to prodding – 'What happened?' 'You were so promising when you were young!' 'I bet you're absolutely exhausted!' 'I like that bit when you…' 'Ha, ha, I saw you when you forgot…' Not to have a protective covering – a mask – is to invite trouble. My actor's mask includes the way I project my voice and intonate my character's words. It is part of my technique for being heard and understood at a distance. However, these vocal devices can become so much a part of me myself, that when I voice an opinion off-stage, my sincerity may be in question. And then, the more I try to emphasise the truthfulness of what I am saying, the more unbelievable I sound. That is the Cassandra effect.

Marianne and I were fortunate because we felt so secure within the confines of our own theatre that we virtually discarded our masks. However, when not on home territory, this could change.

Sometimes, circumstances forced me to swap masks and on one memorable occasion I became very confused as a result. This was during the early seventies, when we had taken *The Bear* round the theatres of Scotland and the north of England as part of an evening's entertainment. Contrary to many people's expectations of Chekhov, *The Bear* is a hilarious farce about a furious, protracted argument between a landowner, Smirnov, and the widow of an old friend of his who has died owing money. The widow, Popova, refuses to pay her dead husband's debts and Smirnov refuses to leave without being paid. After an exchange of insults, Popova accepts Smirnov's challenge to a duel with pistols, whereupon he falls madly in love with her and carries her off. At this point, the curtain comes down, leaving both actors and audience breathless.

One afternoon, we arrived in Kilmarnock in central Scotland to perform in front of five hundred schoolchildren – a daunting prospect at the best of times. We got through the first part of the show successfully. After the interval, we only had to play *The Bear* before taking a rest and re-setting for the evening performance, which was to be played to adults.

I stood in the wings, working myself into a fine fury prior to going on stage and confronting Popova. I concentrated on everything that made me angry in real life – the cost of petrol, the Highlands and Islands Development Board, Scottish education, lack of laundry facilities while on tour, MacBrayne's Ferries. I could hear Marianne, dressed in widow's weeds, refusing to be comforted by the servant, Luka, played by Trina Crichton. No matter how hard the servant tries, Popova keeps harking back to the times she would watch her husband riding his beloved horses. Marianne would then flick Trina with her black-edged handkerchief and there would be a laugh.

On this occasion, the laugh was different; there was a hint of salaciousness in it. I pricked up my ears.

'Oh, how wonderfully he rode!' came Marianne's voice. This time, the laugh was downright dirty; it came from the gallery. From then on, each time riding was

Barrie and Marianne in and out of character in Bill Manhoff's The Owl and the Pussy Cat

mentioned, the obscene guffaws got louder. The feelings of bad temper I was trying to capture took hold of me in earnest. Suddenly, anticipating my entrance by at least a minute, I strode on stage. I was no less surprised by my precipitate action than Marianne and Trina.

Reaching stage-centre, I shouted up to the ribald crew in the gallery, 'We are discussing horsemanship.' My voice was definitely that of Smirnov, not my own. 'We are talking about riding horses,' I continued, as if addressing the whole of the Czar's army, 'not about fucking!'

Silence! The wicked word had turned five hundred children to stone.

I continued, 'Electrician, will you please put on the house lights so that we can see exactly where these unseemly laughs are coming from!' *I* was embarrassed, but Smirnov was thoroughly enjoying himself. As the lights illuminated the auditorium, I saw a sea of expectant, wide-eyed children, sitting stock still, waiting for – what? Then I saw, in the front few rows, a contingent from a girls' school. A 'nice' girls' school. Every one of them looked so anxious that, as I walked off, I found myself apologising to them, still in the character of Smirnov, a somewhat anglicised Bear: 'Sorry, and all that. Had to discipline the guttersnipes in the gallery. Sure you understand!'

Back in the wings, I listened to Marianne as she picked up the scene – which she did with great ease. My interruption had infuriated her and she carried this energy into the rest of the play. When it came to slapping me in the face, she did so with unprecedented force; and at the end, when she had to kiss me passionately, unseen by the audience she stamped as hard as she could on my foot.

Neither of us looked forward to meeting the teachers after the show; but we need not have worried. They all agreed I had done the right thing and confided that they had often wanted to treat the hooligan element in their schools as the Bear had done.

Many years previously, I had behaved just as badly as the children in Kilmarnock. I was on a school outing at a production of Sophocles' *Œdipus Rex*, with Donald Wolfit in the leading role. In my child-like way, unmoved by the great actor and unable to accept the truth of his performance, I found his bleeding face and howls of pain unbelievably funny. On hearing my unrestrained giggles, Wolfit stopped acting and stepped down to the footlights. He picked me out from the audience and reprimanded me in a way I was never to forget. Having been made to feel both very small and rather special at the same time, this had been a lesson to be treasured and followed.

12

Home and Abroad

Although the guesthouse business had now reached a point where holiday-makers were returning regularly and there were good prospects ahead, it was impossible to run it alongside the theatre without damage to both ventures. Regretfully, therefore, we closed the guesthouse in 1970 and concentrated all our efforts on the theatre.

The once cosy guestrooms were quickly transformed into backstage. Although the shops on Mull were remarkably well-stocked, it was not always possible to get what we wanted. So, as a precaution, we never threw anything away… just in case. Space that had accommodated whole families on holiday were now filled with potentially useful things – attractive pieces of wood, plastic bottles, bits of bent metal, pots of paint, lanterns, sound equipment, trunks full of clothes and boxes of costume jewellery. One bedroom was made over into a darkroom, which was fun for all of us. We each took a hand in producing the publicity material and became adept at loading film into the camera, running off seventy or eighty pictures, developing them and then mounting the best results on posters, programmes and newsletters. Another of the bedrooms got emptied out and turned into an office. The old washroom, that had once held a fine boiling copper, became a carpentry store and workshop. It was here that we constructed all the stage props and painted the scenery.

There were times when, as I worked in there, I was transported in memory to the whitewashed cellar in my Aunt Gertrude's house in Buxton. As a very small boy, I had experienced Monday morning wash-days as magical, operatic affairs. Indeed, I can picture the scene now: mist rises from a huge, wood-fired boiler in the corner, blanketing everything except the brightly burning sticks under the great copper. Glimpses of ruddy, sweating flesh belonging, as it might have been, to the Valkyrie in Valhalla. Gertrude and her sisters, my mother amongst them – large, big-breasted and vocal – sang at the tops of their voices: folk songs and arias and then – 'Mind yourself, Barrie,' as they heaved scalding bed linen from the boiling water to the flat stone sink beneath the cellar window, its pane green with algae. Banished from this underwater world, I stood and stared at the doorway. I knew my mother and her sisters were in fact solid and comfortable. But they would sometimes disappear into the swirling vapours and become ethereal creatures from the lands of mythology and fairy tale.

At that age, I had not yet heard of Wagner's operas, but my mother had told me about the Norse legends along with those from Ancient Greece. All sorts of characters played out their mythological existence within the theatre of my head, jostling indiscriminately for partners. The Rhine Maidens danced with Felix the Cat to the music of the suicide's song from *The Mikado*. This had often been sung at my request by my Uncle Raymond and, in the light of his own suicide when I was nineteen, I sometimes wondered about the effect the song had had upon him. My teddy, Pooh Bear, conferred with Poo Bah; Cinderella went to the ball in a boat rowed by the Water Rat; Wotan had tea with the Little Match-Girl; Puss-in-Boots outwitted Cerberus. My mother and aunts, when their too, too solid flesh melted away in the steam from the wash, joined ranks with the wicked dwarf that I had once seen fading away into a cliff face during a transformation scene in a pantomime.

Magical worlds – and not entirely benign. I was frequently kept awake by the reappearance of that wicked dwarf. His face would emerge from my bedroom curtains and, as they wafted gently to and fro, his expression changed. Worse, when there were stronger gusts blowing through the window, he invaded my room, ready to leap on to the bed… but teasingly, he never actually did. He could only be exorcised when an adult smoothed out the creases that formed his features.

It was a good day when my mother showed me how to construct model theatres and make my own devils out of cloth – devils which I could control. The best of these model sets I made from empty shoe-boxes. Using papier-mâché, plasticine and a coloured torch, I conjured up the phantoms that had hitherto been my masters; they were now my slaves. My mother, always helpful when it came to making things, drew up programmes for the scene I had invented and painted little posters with my name topping the bill. Through the medium of shoe-box theatre, I was penetrating mysteries and dispelling childhood fears. Each successive model involved a technical advance. They abounded in lighting effects, trick doors and special magical 'contraptions' – this was a carpetbag word used by small boys at that time. Out of a 'contraption', we devised mechanical answers to all the problems of the universe. And here, busily at work in a scene dock adapted from an old wash-house, I felt myself to be a humble follower of Daedalus, first inventor of the paraphernalia that brought technology to mythology.

In the early seventies, arts societies mushroomed, especially in the north of Britain. Almost overnight, we found ourselves in a seller's market. Happily for us, just when the government was beginning to commit large sums of money to the arts, the Mull Little Theatre was building quite a reputation for itself. Now, full of renewed enthusiasm and dedication, we were able to focus our attention purely on making a success of the theatre.

Touring was not our favourite occupation and, as we had foreseen, it ate into rehearsal time; this meant that the best we could do often had to go by the board. Nevertheless, there were compensations. If the audience applauded long and warmly, we could look forward to returning to the same venue the following year. If, however, the show had gone badly and our reception had been lukewarm, we could escape quickly, be on the road again, leaving the disaster behind us. Although we conscientiously issued detailed address lists, we travelled between one place and another secure in the knowledge that, bar emergencies, nobody except our children and those immediately responsible for them while we were away, knew or cared where we were. We felt very free. Gleefully, the gypsy in us responded to the 'here today, gone tomorrow' lifestyle.

After two years of making short sorties into the outback of Scotland and northern

England, it was possible to contemplate an extended tour all over Britain. We undertook the first of these more ambitious expeditions in a Bedford van given to the theatre by the Michael Marks Charitable Trust.

It was always our intention to start out from Mull in the first weeks of January and aim to return home at the beginning of April. With two or three exceptions, this was the pattern we adhered to over a period of twelve years. We performed in halls, theatres, large living rooms, art galleries and pubs. The average distance between one venue and the next was a hundred miles and, try as we might, we never could arrange the stop-offs in a logical sequence. Our tacks criss-crossed, often doubling back on themselves as we journeyed from place to place; from on high, no doubt they looked like the frenzied wanderings of a crazy insect.

Here are the first entries in the Mull Little Theatre diaries covering a tour we began in the Outer Hebrides in 1971:

Stornoway. The Hotel. £3 5s. B&B. After the show, we were in great need of sandwiches and coffee. Got no service, so I leant a chair against the bell and it rang for half an hour before a girl arrived. She stood in the doorway, giggled, turned on her heels and went away again. We waited another quarter of an hour but still no service. Ended up picnicking in our bedroom on crushed biscuits and bruised apples rescued from the bottom of Marianne's capacious handbag. The hotel didn't provide any towels.

... Something very exciting has happened. We've been given the Scottish Television Award for Services to Scottish Theatre. Celebrated with a haggis supper.

... Tonight we walked into the Harbour Arts Centre in Irvine to find there was no dressing room, no water and no loo.

The 'swings and roundabouts' effect was never more apparent than when we were on tour. We played the town of Crieff several times, the last occasion coinciding with the start of the miners' strike which brought down Edward Heath's government. Had it not been for the timely intervention of Sir William Murray, a local landowner with a passion for theatre, I doubt whether the Mull Little Theatre would have survived the course. As soon as he heard that the strike was likely to put an end to our tour, he told us not to despair: he would lend us a Honda generator, dozens of electric light bulbs with fittings and hundreds of feet of cable.

Armed with this equipment, we gave the theatre organisers along the road plenty of encouragement to 'carry on'; because if they were willing to have a go, so were we. In this way, eleven of the thirteen threatened performances were saved. Audiences turned up determined to enjoy themselves, carrying thermos flasks, blankets and flashlights. There was a feeling of war-time camaraderie about the whole venture.

'Home again, home again, clippety-clop!' is a phrase from the days when Marianne would sing lullabies to the children. At the end of each tour, as we swung in through our white gates, drove round the tight bend past the theatre and drew up in front of the house, I always enjoyed hearing Marianne sing out the old refrain, 'Home again, home again…'

Nevertheless, we were very soon reminded that being on our own territory was not always wine and roses. Running a theatre surrounded by some of the most beautiful countryside in Britain brought its own challenges, especially when the weather was humid. Such conditions brought out the creepy-crawlies.

Frogs would hop across the dressing-room floor and if they weren't spotted and caught they would kerflop-kerflop on to the stage. Toads, disturbed, might stumble out from behind the full-length dressing-room mirror or squat, throats pulsing and jewelled eyes blinking, surprised and surprising amongst the changes of shoes on the rush-matting beneath our rack of costumes. The warm, moist air of summer engendered enormous brown snails. These mammoth creatures left silver trails on the curtain surround of the stage.

Under normal conditions, I could never pick up snails or spiders or things of that nature. However, in front of an audience, I was transformed from mouse into man. If a creepy-crawly fell from the rafters on to the set, scurried on stage from under the floor boards or squelched in from the garden, all my squeamishness vanished. Slug, snail, spider, grass snake, lizard, let them all come! We'd stop the action of the play and I'd scoop up whatever it might be into my hands, say a word to the audience by way of excuse, leave the stage, and unceremoniously throw it out through the door before returning to the acting area.

There's a well-known saying in the theatre: 'Never act with animals or children – they steal the show'. To this I would add, 'Never act with creepy-crawlies – they kill it dead!' This is especially true in an intimate theatre, where the audience can become obsessively worried about whether and when they are going to be crawled over next.

Audiences were quite likely to meet with other hazards during a visit to the Mull Little Theatre and one August, Jim and I managed to save everyone from an extremely unpleasant experience. The main drain from the house became blocked and nasty things began squelching out of the air-vent where visitors to the theatre had parked their cars. This was an emergency. We set to with spades and pickaxes to dig out the drainpipes. By listening to the variations in sound when we hit a pipe with a hammer, we identified the ones which were blocked solid. I broke a hole in the pipe nearest to me and tried to clear it with flexible rods. Jim connected his high-pressure subaqua air-tanks to a hose and attempted to blow out the blockage from high up the hill. We began hearing massive, subterranean rumblings and bubblings. It sounded promising, but nothing happened.

Bravely, Jim stripped off his shirt and put his arm in a polythene bag. Then, grasping a piece of foam rubber to act as a plunger, he stood above the air-vent and, using his full force, drove down hard and fast. His arm went into the pipe – like a piston – right up to the shoulder. There was an almighty explosion, the section in front of my face ruptured and I was drenched in a shower of shard and unspeakable filth. Jim could barely contain himself for laughing: I was covered from head to foot. I wasn't allowed into the house until he had hosed me down.

We all took turns at 'policing' the cars, lining them up compactly but also making sure that car doors did not open on to cow-pats and sheep-pellets. Parking was never easy but, with caution, twenty vehicles could be manoeuvred on to the strip of flat ground immediately in front of the house. We only ever lost one car over the edge of our little hill; and this was pulled back on to the road by a tractor driven by a neighbourly farmer.

Occasionally, late in the season, when it was just Marianne and myself running the show on our own, we had to improvise as best we could if someone arrived after curtain-up. I particularly remember those evenings when we performed *The Four Poster* by Jan de Hartog. With Marianne in a nightie and me in a nightshirt, both snuggled down between the sheets prior to Marianne turning on the master switch (discreetly hidden in the bed), there'd be nothing else for it: one of us would have to get up as we were, walk off stage and go to welcome the visitors.

There is no gainsaying that emergencies of this nature could occasionally bring out the worst in us. We were both temperamental. Too much so, some would say. It was a trait that could manifest in tantrums and petty-mindedness. The continual confusion over the boundaries between our private and public lives fuelled the moments when we were liable to snarl.

Naturally, it was in our interests to keep this waywardness in check. By doing so, we got to know many members of the audience individually and benefited from their contact and friendship. However, at the other end of the spectrum, there were those whom we dreaded coming to the theatre. In that case, we had to work terribly hard to pin a smile on our faces, which was only possible if we admitted openly to ourselves that it wasn't their friendship we were after but their money. They were the people we had tried time and again to woo and win over, but found so dull and dry of spirit that in their presence our efforts to entertain soaked away like water into sand. It got to the point that when the difficult ones wanted to book seats, we'd find an excuse to put them off. From bitter experience, we had learnt to distinguish the regular flame-snuffers. On the phone we would say, 'Oh, how nice to hear from you! You want seats for tonight? Hold on a moment while I check the bookings... I'm most frightfully sorry, but we're absolutely full for tonight! When else could you come? Yes, booked out for that night too... isn't it a shame!' And the shade of Cassandra would leer at me.

A performer is very quick to pick up information from the audience. It doesn't take much – a breath, a little laugh, a sigh, a cough in the right place (or, indeed, the wrong one), a rustle of cloth as a limb moves – each is enough to give an actor what he needs. A good audience offers the performer something to play against and work towards; and this includes – must include – adverse feelings. It is the actor who carries the can for the evening's entertainment; he or she is the one up front, expected to respond to the audience and give them their money's worth.

One glorious evening – when everything went wonderfully well and the audience had responded very enthusiastically, clapping loudly and stamping their feet – quite spontaneously, we clapped them. After that, we nearly always did it, showing our appreciation of the audience by applauding them. Sometimes we clapped with a little less verve than usual. Only rarely, when the audience was very dull, did we not clap them, but bowed instead. This was unfair because, notwithstanding our feelings regarding unresponsive members of the audience, we both firmly believed that it is always the duty of the performer to entertain. Nevertheless, fair or not, it was immensely satisfying to indicate our displeasure after we had played 'to the morgue'.

In a small theatre, actors can assess the emotional 'colour' of almost everyone in the audience and as performers, it is our job to nurture those whose colours are subdued. Within any audience, there are some people who work like yeast; they can be either expansive or quiet in manner – that is not what matters. What counts is their capacity to enthuse those around them. Even in a large theatre, it is easy to pick out such people and play especially to them, thereby exciting a kind of emotional co-operation in warming up those who are slower to respond.

Although we often found ourselves engaged in missionary work, we only really liked playing to the converted. Maurice Wood, one-time Bishop of Norwich, was a convert – the theatrical kind. He and his family regularly visited Mull on holiday and we always enjoyed having them in the audience.

Maurice gets particularly high marks for his appreciation of our priorities. Early one week, he had come to the theatre when we were playing a comedy. He himself was obviously enjoying the show, but we noticed that he seemed to be having an unfavourable impact on the rest of the audience. From the stage, we could see that he was sporting a huge crucifix made from real nails. It commanded a great deal of attention as it rested on his chest, rising and falling in phase with his laughter. We were certain that it had been this stark emblem of his God's sacrifice that had caused the gloom around him. Diffidently, we suggested that he slip this blazing badge of Christianity under his vest on his next visit because, we explained, we could not compete with its overwhelming power. Later that week, he came back to another performance, the crucifix no longer in evidence. This time, the audience was palpably at ease.

There were, of course, many times when the audience gave us back as good as they got. One particular evening, sitting in the front row, there was a woman we knew to be very deaf. Accordingly, we projected our voices more than usual, sending most of the play in her direction. During a dramatic pause – one of those exquisite moments when everyone was holding their breath and Marianne and I had the play poised between us like a piece of delicate porcelain – she announced in a loud voice to the friend sitting beside her, 'Can't hear a word. Why don't they speak up?'

On another occasion, we were performing a little Edwardian farce called *Packing Up* by Harry Grattan There was a fine figure of a man sitting not three feet away from the stage in the front row, wearing a kilt. Whenever there was anything funny, he positively shook with laughter, slapping his bare knee as he roared. Some extra bit of stage business that Marianne had slipped into her performance caught his eye. Whereupon, he went into a paroxysm of laughter, missed his aim and brought down his mighty hand in a thundering smack on the knee of the lady sitting next to him. She nearly jumped out of her skin with surprise and it was only by dint of tremendous self-control on our part that we were able to continue with the play.

13

Dispatches

An entry from my diary for 1976 reads:

Tuesday, 25 May: Tonight is the opening night of the new season. This morning, Marianne cut my hair and I trimmed hers. Made two hundred chocolate cakes; cleaned the foyer and set the plays; oiled the curtain pulleys; ran lines. Bagged up the cakes and put them in the deep freeze. Duplicated the minutes for the previous Directors' Meeting and posted them to members of the Theatre Board. By 11 o'clock in the morning, this evening's performance is booked out... By 8.30 p.m., Pauline (our front-of-house lady), in her inimitable way, has squeezed in the patrons and got them sitting in the least likely places so we were playing to many more than a full house. She cajoled them on to the window-sill, the cold, concrete steps (we never insured against patrons getting an attack of piles) and, for the more fortunate, there were cushions brought in from the main house.

Pauline had the knack of turning every evening at the theatre into a party. The welcome she gave people made our task on stage that much easier because, by the time the audience were seated, they were in a good humour. Even before the curtain went up, those who had come fifty miles from the other end of the island, along appalling single-track roads in dreadful weather, were made to feel it was all worth it. I can think of no one better than her to save us from the theatre manager's nightmare – a double booking. Very occasionally, we made a mistake in this department and would find ourselves in the embarrassing situation of having more people booked in than places to fill. Nevertheless, Pauline always managed to shoehorn them in, one way or another, even if it meant having a member of the audience sitting on stage with us.

The record number of people we squeezed into our tiny auditorium was after I had completely forgotten to write down a booking from a troop of Ranger Scouts. Pauline overcame any potential upset by having them all sit on the floor right at the very front. As we walked on stage, we saw a long line of heavy walking boots sticking out at us from under the closed curtain. Just as we were about to begin the show, four more people turned up. They had come all the way from Israel to see us, and had been misinformed by a tourist agent on the mainland that there was no need to book. 'Can we turn them away?' Pauline asked. The audience, in true pantomimic fashion, sent up a great cry of 'No!' 'Can we make room for them?' 'Yes!' Usually, we seated thirty-seven. With extra chairs, we could often manage forty-two; but that evening it was fifty-eight.

The season continued with the theatre doing reasonably good business which gave us a little freedom to try out new ways of presentation without fear of frightening off

Barrie and Marianne on stage addressing the audience at the end of the show

the punters and thereby losing income. Even so, because our economy was marginal, anything we attempted had to be on a modest scale.

For instance, there was the 'Newspaper Theatre'. I believe the idea for this had originated in New York between the wars. From the moment I first heard about it from an American when I was a student in London, I had wanted to try it out. The form it took in the Mull Little Theatre could hardly have been simpler. Twice a week, I would write and present a short duologue about local politics for a pair of tendentious Highland worms, Iain and Angus. Since the ideal time for their first appearance was during the break between some short, light-hearted comedies by the Hungarian playwright, Ferenc Molnár, all I had to decide on was the format. This was more or less dictated by whatever resources we had to hand which were, as usual, rather scanty.

After improvising with a couple of ideas, we found a way to bring Iain and Angus to life. First, Marianne unpicked two seams in the front stage curtains, just enough for me to get my hands through into the auditorium with room to manipulate the puppets. These I had created out of a pair of ankle socks adorned with eyes and mouths made from brightly coloured felt. I gave Iain a gruff voice and Angus a squeak. Then, while the scenery was being changed around me, and with the script either held up in front of me or pinned to the curtain at eye-level, I would pop the puppets through their worm-holes and begin: 'How are you, the day, Iain?' 'Fine, fine…and yourself, Angus?' 'Fine, or I would be were it not for my neighbour, the Red Tape Worm…' and so on. Any subject that the local community found particularly irritating was fair game for the Worms. However, I soon discovered that writing even a short, satirical script could be very wearing. What is more, I had not anticipated the popularity of the Worms, nor the personalised response they received. I was often approached by local people and asked to join in with this or that cause; or – which could be very tempting but also very dangerous – to side with one or other party in a quarrel. Conflict and scandal are powerful elements in keeping up publicity; but I was determined to avoid such hazardous involvement and, after a very successful two-year run, Iain and Angus were 'rested'.

There was also our *Punch and Judy*. This, like so much of what happens in the theatre, grew out of something personally experienced long before. When I was about fifteen years old, my Uncle Raymond had announced that he was taking me to Manchester to see a *Punch and Judy* show. I was appalled. Fifteen and being taken to a kids' show! Whatever next? But I didn't say anything because in the past my uncle

Backstage at the sound consol setting up for Chekhov's Tatyana Repin

hardly ever failed to come up trumps when he planned expeditions. Any misgivings I may have had on this occasion proved to be completely unfounded.

The diminutive hand puppets, with their outsize heads and flapping arms, played out their deadly drama in a traditionally striped booth, before a large audience of children and adults. This was a five-star production which deserved an 'H'-rating for Horror. From the moment Mr Punch appeared, he seemed to take us all by the throat and shake the emotions out of us. Laughing and joking in a ghastly squeaky voice, he killed with a ruthlessness that was truly amazing – babies, wife, policeman, judge, jury, crocodile, all murdered as he crowed, 'That's the way to do it!' Most significantly, the play ended with Mr Punch triumphant. Here was no sentimental tale for children, but a cynical view of the adult world. It was an horrific vision and, because it had been such a powerful theatrical experience, it stayed with me over the years.

A happy chance on tour jolted my memory of that day in Manchester and gave me a reason for creating our own Mr Punch. We had arrived in the attractive Yorkshire town of Whitby and were taking time out before the evening performance to browse through the bookshops. Marianne and I went our different ways; when we met up again, she proudly showed me a second-hand copy of the script of a children's version of *Punch and Judy*. As for me, all I had was that day's edition of *The Guardian*. I turned the leaves of the little book while Marianne read an article I had pointed out in the paper because I found it interesting. It was about Idi Amin's cruel régime in Uganda. The coincidence pointed the way forward: we had found what we needed and knew exactly what we had to do for our next experimental production.

The theme was sombre – corrupt government, cruelty and cupidity – and it was essentially a puppet play for adults. The voices were recorded and the puppets were as grotesque as we could make them. My own favourite was the judge, a death's head, constructed out of the skull of a sheep that I'd picked up on the hill behind the house. When it came to audience response, we noticed that although the men in the audience laughed uncomfortably at Mr Punch (who was the epitome of male chauvinism), the women were too disturbed by his rapaciousness to get much enjoyment from him. Needless to say, the children loved the whole thing and wanted more.

It was at about this time that we had received a request from Richard Demarco, the Edinburgh entrepreneur, to bring twenty-five people to the theatre. His secretary rang to confirm the booking and tell us that all was well – indeed, better than ever – he would be bringing not twenty-five but thirty-five visitors. This, I thought, was typical of Ricky, for ever the optimist. We had accepted the booking with mixed feelings which turned out to be quite justified; the arrangement played havoc with our other bookings and, as it turned out, with our co-ordination as actors.

Marianne had prepared a little anthology specially for them, based on the first programme we ever presented in the theatre. When we came to the Kate and Petruchio quarrel from *The Taming of the Shrew*, Marianne hit me as usual, lightly but in such a

On tour in Wales

way that it made plenty of noise. For the very first time, she missed her aim and the heel of her hand landed on the point of my jaw. The slap, despite its lightness, managed to knock me out. My legs crumpled beneath me, I lost my lines and began to speak gibberish. I could hear people laughing, including Marianne, but I had no idea what they were laughing at.

On 12 July the same year, we were working on tour letters – Marianne at one desk and I at another. It was after six in the evening and I needed a cup of tea. I got up to stretch and walked over to Marianne. She smiled up at me, then suddenly her face contorted into a mask of fury. She attacked me physically, very hard, but because the blows hit me on the chest, I wasn't hurt. As she continued to thump me, her expression changed to one of disbelief, as though she herself could not understand the vehemence of the onslaught. There was nothing I could do but hold her close until she calmed down.

'What was that about?' I asked. 'I haven't the faintest,' she answered.

'Why did you want to hit me?' 'It wasn't you,' she replied.

Later on that evening, there was a call from the hospital in Tooting in London to tell us that her mother had died at 6.30 p.m., the very moment that Marianne had turned on me.

Grief is a taboo subject and I often think that this is where the Victorians had the advantage over us. At least they knew what grief was about, what to expect of it. Neither Marianne nor I were prepared for its effects upon us.

For some months following her mother's death, Marianne's moods swung violently; I felt as though she had dragged me on to the big dipper at a fairground. Before I had time to catch my breath, she was back on top of the world. But not for long. She slammed into reverse and, holding my hand, down the slope she'd go. I grew extremely worried for her and feared her health might crack up altogether; but she continued to learn lines, write letters, organise the business as efficiently as ever and perform well.

There were other ways in which we coped with the sadness. For example, noticing that there were not enough items for sale in the foyer for children, Marianne got out her bag of bits and pieces and set about making bright, cheerful dinosaurs out of felt off-cuts. My contribution was a dozen hand-made boomerangs – after all, there was plenty of space on Mull to try them out.

The Mull Little Theatre itself had healing powers and continued to work its magic. In fact, it proved to be quite a matchmaker. Many couples were brought together through its benign influence. There were those who met by chance in the foyer, found they had things in common and went on to build a relationship.

The magic was at its most potent when there was a spell of appalling weather – for choice, pelting rain and a remorseless wind. Under such conditions, there was always the likelihood of a minor camping disaster: theatre patrons who had been washed out of their tents would reappear in the foyer to ask if we could help get their clothes dry. The least we could do on these occasions was to hang their dripping things over the kitchen hoist and offer them the stage to sleep on.

The lucky few who had had to abandon their camp site when *The Four Poster* was in repertory got the best deal of all. While the wind howled, damp leaves stroked the slates and raindrops pattered down outside, a couple would keep dry and snug between the sheets of an ornate mock-up of a nineteenth-century four-poster bed. A single stage lantern imparted a comfortable glow from the rafters above – a glint of surprise pink on the white-washed walls and surrounding velvet curtains. Marianne and I never slept there ourselves, but we were told it was a perfect love-nest. Twice we received assurances that a child was conceived as the result of a couple spending a night in our theatre.

Our 1976 tour was the longest we ever undertook and it was Nick's turn to be our stage manager. We had arranged with a young woman, Fiona Allen, to be our driver. We got off the island in good time but the crossing was vicious; the ship's stabilisers were not working and she pitched and rolled so violently that all the shelving in the van collapsed. It was as though we had been hit by a small explosion; costumes, stage props, lanterns and valuable sound equipment lay in a chaotic heap on the floor of the van. Once we had reached dry land again, we tore out all the shelving and threw it away. Having completely repacked it and hoping that we would meet no worse mishap, we were ready to face the forthcoming 6,000-mile trek.

The first part of the journey was very short. It took us to Tayvallich, a picturesque village set between a loch and the sea – a place tucked away in the hills so secretly that I could easily believe it to be the natural source of all the weird and wonderful stories of Highland life. After the show in the village hall, we found great comfort in staying that first night with the remarkable Dowager Lady Gainford. She met us with welcoming smiles, large drinks and a delectable dinner of pork with olives. After the upsetting journey, when everything seemed to go wrong, she was like a fairy godmother who put all to rights.

In the North, we made landfall at Yell, the penultimate island of the Shetlands; in the South, we reached the Isle of Wight. Between these two points on the map, we took in over 60 dates and were on the move for three months. To begin with, the weather was appalling. The journey to Stirling was particularly hair-raising; there was black ice on the road, thunder and lightning and flurries of blinding snow driven by a high wind. The van slid all over the place. The next venue, Strathaven, was cut off by road so we had to pack what we could in a trunk and then, having left the van with friends in Blairlogie, travel to our destination by train.

A few days later, when the weather conditions had improved, we were back on the road driving to Arisaig in the Highlands. Finding ourselves far from anywhere, with the petrol running low, we stopped at an isolated filling station in the middle of a blasted heath. 'Can we have five gallons?' we enquired.

The attendant replied in the soft dialect of Inverness, 'I'll ask the boss.' He disappeared behind a shack and shouted to someone, 'Are we open for petrol?' The reply that wafted back to us on the icy air was an eldritch screech, as if the surrounding gneiss rock had given voice, 'No. Not at all. We don't *feel* open the day!'

We continued southwards to play in the north-east of England. It was getting colder. In the interval during a show at Tynemouth, Fiona complained of feeling very sleepy.

We were not surprised. After all, even though Nick was taking on some of the driving as a learner, she had had a long drive. Then her eyes began to drift up and her breathing slowed down dramatically. I rushed on stage and addressed the audience, using a phrase I thought could only be used by a character in a film, 'Is there a doctor in the house?' By good chance, there was. He took a quick look at Fiona and diagnosed hypothermia. Luckily, too, there were plenty of theatre curtains about: we wrapped her up in them until she had all but disappeared. We plied her with lots of hot, sweet tea and she slowly recovered. After a good night's sleep, she was able – and very determined – to carry on.

Our journey took us northwards again. Before we started the show that evening, our sound equipment gave us some trouble. Nick traced the fault to the Bang and Olafsen tape-recorder, which had taken some heavy knocks. He mended it by saturating the whole thing in Evostick. It struck me that it would be a miracle if it worked again after such dramatic treatment, but it did. 'Or,' as I wrote in my diary at the time, 'perhaps we were so high on fumes, it just appeared that it did!'

We doubled back. Our course took us south again to Whitby in Yorkshire and then west to Ulverston, north of the Lake District, to play to 'a lot of kids – totally foul and horrid' (Marianne's comment). From Ulverston we turned right, and then left to Pendlebury, near Manchester. It was near here that a very old lady came up to us after the show and said in a rich Lancashire dialect, 'You were better than television – you were thicker!' We assumed she meant we were three-dimensional.

Touring was such a haphazard, random affair that the old joke – 'What's today?' 'Thursday.' 'Then it must be Oldham!' – came to have a serious meaning. Sometimes all sense of location and time was lost, as if we were travelling in limbo.

It was another death that jerked us out of the spellbound existence that otherwise enveloped us whilst touring. We learnt that Caryl Jenner, who had been our employer when Marianne and I got married, had died. The show still had to go on that evening – a comedy, what is more – against a powerful inclination to give ourselves time to be private with our memories of her.

It was very like another time, just before a performance, when we heard that my favourite aunt, Gertrude, had shuffled off this mortal coil. By coincidence, it was fitting that I received the news the night we played Clitheroe, the little Lancashire town lying at the foot of Pendle Hill – where my aunt's family had originated. An entry in my diary reads:

> I would like time to grieve for her and go to the funeral, but that is impossible. We played in a pub tonight, draping our black curtains over the bar counter to create a dressing room amongst the beer-levers and glasses. The audience was small but appreciative. I had not been looking forward to tonight but we all thoroughly enjoyed ourselves… the healing power of Dr. Theatre!

We were then to do some performances a few miles south of Clitheroe, in and around Blackburn. Our organiser here was a true descendent of Mrs Malaprop. He talked of 'pantomines', with 'Buttins dressed up as Little Lord Fontinroy'. He said of an actress: 'Not a soprano but a – what do you call 'em – a mello… a metro singer.' He agreed with us that Scotland needed its 'evolution'.

We came across many rich characters in this part of the world. I asked one man to tell me exactly where he came from, as I was interested in his dialect. He answered, 'I've got no come-froms but a lot of go-tos.'

One night, we were playing in a small disco hall on the outskirts of Blackburn. We started with three in the audience. Twenty minutes into the play, four more turned up. At the interval, two of the original three walked out, so we were down to five. Two of these were weak in the head and stank of urine – we could smell it from the stage. Shortly after the interval, they quit the building only to return, eating fish and chips (again, the smell was powerful) and whispering so loudly to each other that they drove two others away before they themselves finally left. In the end, the audience consisted of one old lady – clapping enthusiastically all on her own.

By this time, Marianne and I were so tired that we ourselves were ready to drop dead. Nick, who happened to overhear us complaining, said that if we did he would stuff us and tote us round for the rest of the tour, charging people two pence a time for the pleasure of seeing us. At which point, Marianne perked up from where she was sitting at the back of the van and quoted Shakespeare: 'When they will not give a doit to relieve a lame beggar, they will lay out ten to see a dead Indian.'[6]

During this particular tour, the Little Theatre worked its magic again. Marianne and I could not help noticing how well Nick was getting on with Fiona. Some years later, they got married and now still live in Scotland with their two children.

6 *The Tempest*, II.ii.33

14

Rude Mechanicals

January 1978. The film maker, Derek Bailey, at the behest of Scottish Television, is to make a film about our work…

… An invitation to attend the Royal Garden Party at Holyrood Palace. These are exciting times… The first person we met today as we walked in through the Palace gates also came from Mull. She informed us proudly that her very pretty hat cost her 5p at a jumble sale at Salen… Marianne has shingles, and though it is a very small spot, it is just under her bra strap and is driving her mad…

… 19 May. Pussy-Beg, our much loved family cat died today…

My pocket-book diaries, scuffed and coffee-stained, give only a brief account of the daily happenings; and as I flick through the pages, I am aware how fragmented this account of our life and feelings now seems. Nevertheless, mention of the death of Pussy-Beg gives pause for thought about those important neighbours on Mull – the animals with which our family had dealings. The cats in particular contributed so much to the quality of our lives that they deserve a chapter all to themselves.

Enter, then, the country folk, dancing! A heavy-footed jig, presented by the field rats – dark grey fellows, rarely seen, but most definitely often heard. They set up their music and rumpus in the cavities behind our bedroom walls. They would scuttle and bang about, as though they had clogs on, for ever moving in and out with all their worldly possessions loosely crated in heavy wooden boxes and old, creaking theatre skips – making an enormous racket. Every night they held a frolicsome junketing – that is, until Pussy-Beg joined the family.

She came to us, a little smoky ball of fluff, as a gift from a beautiful young Highland lass whose calm demeanour all but persuaded us that she was from Tir nan Og, speaking the language of the fairy folk. Pussy-Beg, the prima ballerina, was deaf in both ears. Her disability had far-reaching effects on her behaviour, and as with some humans, her deafness did not improve her character. Dogs could bark themselves into a fit, but she wouldn't notice them or budge. The older she got, the deafer she became, and the more crabbed and awkward. She developed a foghorn voice, presumably to hear herself; and, because her stentorian tones could wake even the deepest of sleepers, she exerted absolute power. On frequent occasions, there I'd be, slipping a mackintosh over my pyjamas and traipsing out into the wet to pick up this howling banshee of a cat. There was quite simply no alternative. If I hadn't fetched her in, the residents, our guests, would have lost sleep and we might have lost their custom. Against all the odds, Pussy-Beg had quickly inveigled herself into our affections and we couldn't possibly get rid of her; besides which, she was an excellent ratter.

Her partner – her stage-door Johnny – couldn't make her out at all. He was known in the village by the name of Smiddypuss, and was a cat to inspire legends. He'd been left as a tiny, black and white kitten, abandoned in a cardboard box on the local rubbish dump. One of the girls in the village had rescued him; she used to live in the former Dervaig smithy, so this is how he came by his name. When he was strong enough, he had taken off on his own and, for the most part, lived off the land.

It wasn't until we'd been in Druimard for a year that he made his presence known to us. He had eyes like green jewels which sparkled from behind a mat of long hair; his coat was bedecked with leaves and interwoven with yellow and brown bracken. He might have been dressed for the part of a fairy in *A Midsummer Night's Dream*.

When Smiddypuss first came to visit us, he wasn't so much timid as wary. He would shimmy into the kitchen, a Jeeves-like presence, take a plateful of any food we had put down for him – curry was a favourite – then shimmy out again, usually dropping a few sheep-ticks on the way.

He never learnt to behave himself in the house; we were always coming across little puddles or discreet piles. However, like a Shakespearean character, he wore the dignity of great comedy about him and our irritation never lasted long.

He himself was subject to great irritation. Sheep-ticks are parasites that dig into the flesh, suck blood until they grow full, then – when they are about the size of a black pea – drop off. Marianne and I found they favoured the backs of our knees. Both the cats had them embedded in their shoulders and round the tops of their heads. For ourselves, a drop of methylated spirits would kill a tick and cause it to fall out.

When Marianne first stroked Smiddypuss, she put her hand on his head only to find it covered in ticks. She was so horrified at the thought of what they might be doing to him that she grabbed the bottle of methylated spirits which was always to hand and poured it over him. He fled as though he'd been scalded. We imagined we would never see him again. But in three days he was back. He crept in, his body close to the ground, sidled up to Marianne's foot and nudged it. He was telling her something. Gently, she put her hand down to touch his head and, sure enough, there they were again, a scalpful of ticks. While she investigated, he held his ground, making it clear that he was willing to undergo unpleasant medicine to get relief.

It amazes me to think that he had put the shock of the methylated spirits and the loss of the ticks into some kind of cause-and-effect relationship, but that is what he seemed to have done. She got out the bottle and showed it to him. He flinched, but put his head lower and stayed where he was. The spirit flowed on to him; he stuck it for as long as he could, then made for the door like a bat out of hell. For the time being, he could take no more; but from then on, this tick-clearing became a little ritual. We realised we had met Supercat.

Early in her life, Pussy-Beg had been spayed and therefore had no time for Smiddypuss. He tried to woo her but, apart from anything else, she couldn't hear him. This gave him something to consider; he watched her, patiently, much as a naturalist would watch a new species. And, in watching, he learnt from her. He learnt to wash. Never having had a mother cat to care for him, he had missed out on grooming skills.

The first time he saw Pussy-Beg lift her long back leg to wash her nether regions, his interest quickened and I could virtually hear him saying to himself, 'What's she up to now? Can I do that, I wonder?' He tried, but he couldn't. He shot his leg straight into the air, rolled over and fell flat on his back. He practised with great persistence, but he never got it quite right.

What with Pussy-Beg and Smiddypuss, the rats and other vermin hadn't a chance. Nevertheless, we were delighted to find that the local birds lived very happily and actually increased in number. Pussy-Beg took no notice of them whatsoever. On the other hand, Smiddypuss appeared to positively enjoy their company. On hot days, he would lie out under the wide-spreading branches of the beech tree overlooking the kitchen, sunning himself in the dust, letting the little birds hop round him. There'd be a glint in his green eyes as he watched, but that was all. I never knew him to hunt them. For a short while, one of our stage managers introduced two pet cats from his home in the south. The effect was immediate and disastrous to the bird population which was almost wiped out overnight. As soon as the wholly domestic cats left, the birds returned.

It was a joy to watch Smiddypuss hunt. From our living room window, we could observe him sitting still as a stone beside a mouse run or a path taken regularly by field rats. He was patience itself until, suddenly – whap! One strong blow of his paw and that was that. He never played with his quarry. He was too much the professional.

He had a quality about him that was Falstaffian. Although he was not a fat cat, his stomach was often so distended from eating meat that it grazed the floor as he walked. If he tried to run in this bloated condition, his paunch swung from side to side so violently that he would be swung off his feet and have to take time off to sit and rest.

I had always wanted to see him get to work on a rabbit and, one day in summer, I had that opportunity. There came a knock on the door of the hut – this was before we moved back into the main house following the end of a theatre season – and there outside was Hughie Balfour Paul, the son of the local laird. He had with him two recently-killed rabbits that he held up by the ears. As Hughie and I bargained the price, Smiddypuss strolled up and sat on the doormat between us. Then, one of the rabbits relaxed its abdominal muscles and let go a stream of urine. The cat was exhilarated. He leapt forward, lifted his face to catch the full benefit of the golden shower, rolled over on his back, scrambled to his feet again to jump up and down and dance under it.

It was such an extraordinary exhibition, I thought he deserved a reward. So, having bought the pair, I took one of them to a little rise of grass that ran between the hut and the house. I laid the dead rabbit on the bank and before I could say 'knife' Smiddypuss had pushed my hand out of the way with a firm nudge of his hard forehead and, using the sharp heel-claw, ripped the belly open in one quick, clean movement. Then he thrust his head right inside the wound and dragged out the liver with his teeth. One gulp and it was gone. Next, he ripped out the lungs and heart and then, with his head buried in the stomach again, he was after the kidneys. The whole business was conducted with terrifying expertise.

Old Smiddypuss returned to us for many years until one day I caught a glimpse of him crawling into the bushes behind the house. He looked in distress. To my shame, I was too harassed by my own immediate concerns to follow him. He never appeared again.

Several years later, a family of feral cats came to live beside us. I once counted thirteen of them. They were a strain of domestic cat who, for various reasons, over the years, had left the comfort of hearth and home but congregated under our hut for safety and companionship. They had a lovely life, hunting well and sleeping deeply. Soon after they took up possession of the space below the floorboards, we learnt that cats in the wild are very loud snorers. Their nocturnal chorale of rattling grunts and whistles was sometimes loud enough to wake us out of sleep.

Occasionally, these ferals would come to see what was going on at the theatre. We would find them sitting patiently in a queue that stretched from the theatre to the main house. It is quite unnerving to have twenty-six predatory eyes peering at one through the tall grass - especially as each cat had a personality of its own. Of course, we did our best to keep them out of the theatre building, but this was not always possible. A few times, we would find them on stage with us; and the only situation when they were amenable to being picked up and held was while we were acting.

They kept themselves to themselves, accepting our handouts with no grace whatsoever, grabbing what we offered and fleeing with it as if we had been in the habit of beating them regularly. That is, all but one. This was a dainty little quean who carried her tail differently to the others - who trailed theirs along the ground in the manner of the Scottish wild cat. She was always to be found near the house and sometimes in it. Once, on our return from tour, we were saddened to find that she was not part of the cats' welcoming committee. She obviously hadn't had the necessary aggression to make a go of it on the hill.

15

Shivering Shocks

The children were children no longer; they had become young men. We entered that phase of life when parents face making the transition from being a mother or father with a family to being a couple on their own again. For the first time in my life, I caught some of Marianne's self-consciousness about age. Now, when we looked at each other, we saw the 'Victoria and Albert' of Central School twenty-five years on: the brittle faces of our youth, like photographs in a forgotten album, had softened and faded. When Nick announced that he and Fiona were going to get married, we really took stock.

After the wedding, which was held in the south of England, we had returned to Mull to find the communication from Derek Bailey, confirming that he wanted to make a film about us. Bright skies.

Then, on Thursday 27 July 1979, black clouds suddenly 'loured upon our house' and, like something out of a horror film, took on a tangible form, a sense of evil. Marianne and I were undressing in the bedroom after a performance of *The Owl and the Pussy Cat* by Bill Manhoff. Marianne removed her pullover and bra, and stretched her arms above her head. In a typical gesture, she wiggled the tips of her fingers in a dance-like movement towards the ceiling. In this position, she glanced sideways into the mirror.

'Barrie,' she said, 'my breast's got a double chin.' It was a good description of how the gentle curve beneath the nipple was slightly distorted. She cupped her hand under it. 'What's that?' she asked me. 'Feel there. Is there a lump, do you feel a lump? What is it?'

'Better see the doc,' I said. I suddenly felt nervous. It went through my mind that I'd been here before. Wasn't it to do with my Granny Olivia and the intriguing hardness of her hugs all those years ago?

As we stepped out of the house the next morning on our way to the surgery, pale sunshine reflected on her delicate skin. I searched her face very closely for any sign of ill health. She was obviously tired, but that was nothing unusual. We were, after all, in the middle of the season and she was only just getting over an attack of shingles. The doctor did not mince his words. 'I can't tell you what it is, but I don't play about with lumps. I'll have a biopsy arranged for you in Glasgow.'

Back at home, we absorbed as best we could what all this might mean. 'Oh!' said Marianne, 'The film – Derek Bailey – he was going to begin filming this week. You'll have to phone him. Apologise, darling, do apologise.'

After the show that night, I wrote in my diary:

The doctor has moved very fast and arranged for M to go into Ward 33 in the

Glasgow Royal Infirmary next Monday. Tonight we played to a full house. When we came to the final curtain, I could not address the audience out front. It was Marianne who stepped forward to explain that we were closing for a few days but would be open again very soon, so they should watch the local posters. She did not say why; she just mentioned 'things beyond our control'.

We had that Sunday to prepare for her visit to Glasgow. It was not an easy day to get through; the suitcase was soon packed and then all we had to do was wait. We sat on the front step and soaked up the sun. None of the boys were at home; they were all working on the mainland. We discussed whether we should wait until we had definite news one way or the other, before telling them.

Monday arrived. We travelled to Glasgow by train (neither of us had yet learnt to drive) and then by taxi to the Royal Infirmary – the hospital first made famous by the great Scottish surgeon, Lister. It stood towering over us, a huge, blackened, Victorian edifice. Steps, revolving door, hospital smell, oval stairwell, curved landing, right-angled turn, double doors, ward sister, clipboard, yellow curtains, swish! Snapshot impressions.

While Marianne was in hospital I stayed at Blairlogie with friends. Two days later, I wrote:

Well, there it is. The ward sister met me with the words, 'The news is not good.' I tried to look calm and sensible. She went on, 'There is a cancer but, having said that,' she paused and smiled up at me, 'things could not be better. The tumour is very small and there are no complications.' I stood, scarcely breathing... When I took in air, I realised the sister had very gently taken hold of my hand. 'When?' I asked.

I was told the operation was to be in two days' time, on Thursday. I went numb. Then, down the ward, I saw Marianne looking for me. She was in a bright red dressing gown, the one she had worn so often as the madcap hostess in Michael Frayn's farce, *Chinaman*. She waved and smiled cheerfully. Rigid as an automaton, I walked towards her, legs tick-tocking backwards, forwards. As I neared her she said, 'Come on, it's nothing, and the tests tell us that apart from the little lump, I'm A1 healthy!'

I had bought three red carnations from a flower seller standing by the hospital gates. Twice each week, during performances of the love story *Old World* by the Russian author, Alexei Arbuzov, I had given Marianne three of these flowers; but they had been made of plastic. The time had come to give her three real ones. I sat on the bed beside her and gave her the flowers – in public, as I had always done. There were nurses and patients all around us; but this time we could not have felt more alone with each other. 'Bloody hell, why did you do that?' she asked, her eyes filling with tears. 'Because I love you,' I answered. 'Now look what you've done to my make-up!' she said. She wasn't wearing any and it was a silly joke, but it broke the tension.

For a while, we sat looking at each other without speaking. Then she admitted to having been terrified at first. But as the news about it being only a small tumour seeped into her consciousness, she felt better; and now that I was with her, she felt better still. I didn't feel very supportive. I was not crying openly but I felt as if the tears were streaming down the inside of my face – behind the actor's mask. Now we knew the result was positive – and it struck me then how ironic an expression this is for diagnosing disease – it was time to inform our sons.

They each said they would have liked to have been told before she went in for the biopsy, but they also led us to believe that they understood why we had been reticent. I returned to the ward and found her radiant, chatting to everyone and cheering them up. In my absence, she had written a short letter to Arbuzov, telling him about the gift of the three carnations. I felt that perhaps I had been too sentimental in the choice of flowers; but she told me not to be silly – and wasn't the letter proof of her appreciation? It might have been. But I was in need of reassurance too, and not just about the carnations. On leaving the ward that evening, she asked me to buy a dozen boxes of tights for the nurses. 'They are so badly paid and always have to supply their own, yet they always look so neat and tidy,' she said.

The diary continues:

Thursday, 3 August. I am in my bedroom at Blairlogie, sitting on the bed. I find quite the best way for me to keep calm and not let my imagination run away with me is to concentrate on theatre movement exercises by Litz Pisk. It is now 10 a.m. and she is in the operating theatre. Through the window I can see a burgundy-coloured rose emerging out of the thick morning mist…

… Richard travelled up from Newcastle-upon-Tyne to be with me on my first visit after the operation. We saw Marianne from a distance, lying in bed. She looked magnificent! So healthy, and only a little bit woozy from the anaesthetic.

On the window-sill beside her head were enormous bunches of flowers. There was one from the Scottish Arts Council.

(Next day)… She's up and had a shower. She feels great. Jim took me to the Walt Disney film *Pinocchio*; he said it would do me good. It did. Derek Bailey has sent a magnificent bunch of flowers and phoned the ward to reassure Marianne not to feel bad about the cancellation of the film. He told her on the phone that when he rang the hospital to ask if they had Marianne in the ward, the answer in broad Glaswegian was 'Yeees, we doo, and a beeeuat'ful woman she is tuu!' This has put her on top of the world. She is now talking about getting back to acting as fast as she can. As for me, I'm absolutely shattered. Going round Glasgow shopping for her is a marvellous tonic.

A day or two later the entries read:

Marianne has had her prosthesis fitted. It's like a breast made for a humanoid. It's creepy to touch and, disconcertingly, I found holding it quite an erotic sensation. Perhaps because it is not actually attached to a human, there is an element of the pornographic about it, or perhaps I mean fetishistic. I would never have expected to think such a thought about an artificial replacement for my wife's beautiful breast. I have just watched her dance round the ward wearing it. The surgeon was doing his round and, as he crossed from one bed to another, she caught hold of his hand and danced with him. He was quite taken aback – Glasgow for aye, say I!

She is to have radiotherapy, but not immediately. Her surgeon says she can wait until the end of the theatre season. He, too, is keen to get her back on stage. That will be good for our morale.

Friday, 11 August. I can take her home! She was over the moon. Furthermore, there was something in her voice I had never heard before: she sounded markedly Cockney. Jim, Nick and Fiona drove over to get us. On the journey home, Nick asked if he might see the wound. Marianne opened up her blouse, and we saw the neat stitches and strappings across her flat chest. Nick looked for some time at where the breast had been and then said, 'What a shame, it's like throwing out a valuable piece of family furniture!' Marianne loved that and quoted it often.

Tuesday, 14 August. It's only eleven days since the operation and yet, last night, Marianne performed in *Village Wooing*, which we've brought back into repertory. When I got to the line, 'We shall light up a lamp in the holy of holies of life for one another,' I was suddenly overwhelmed with gratitude. How fortunate we were to be back and acting together again. I found it hard to speak; for a moment I stopped 'lighting the lamp'. I stopped acting. Marianne saw me falter and looked daggers at me, as if to say, 'This is not an appropriate moment to go sentimental on me!'

The show was a huge success. Everyone in the audience knew what had happened. I was conscious that most of the audience, at one time or another, might try to guess her secret by identifying which breast was real and which was false. This was an uncharitable thought which was put to flight as soon as I recognised the warmth being directed towards Marianne on stage… I'm writing this sitting on the edge of the bath, waiting for her to get out so that I can dry her. She still feels a bit unsure on her feet… We inspected the wound together and she wept over the mutilation.

Marianne was determined not to be beaten by the cancer and, having always had a weather-eye for publicity, she was saying, 'I've got cancer – let's use it, turn it to our account.' Even before she was out of hospital, she argued that we must take full advantage of the peculiar quirk of human nature which makes people respond favourably to a crisis.

I remember her standing in front of the dressing-room mirror at a time when the prognosis was not good, trying on hats for a comedy part. As she slipped on a black toque – which gave her a distinctly horsy look – she mused to herself and referred to that favourite quote of hers, 'It's no use whipping a dead horse, but you can flog a dead Indian. So, if you've got a dying horse,' and here she pulled a long face at me, 'stick

Marianne in close-up, 1979

feathers on it!' Whereupon, she swapped the toque for a befeathered head-dress and grinned at me. I did not know how to respond to this; there were times when her pragmatism verged on cynicism and, like a cold shower, took my breath away.

Marianne realised that there was publicity to be made out of her illness – for women's health, the promotion of cancer research, as well as for the theatre. She used the few minutes after each show when we announced 'forthcoming attractions' to inform audiences about what had happened to her. She told them how fit she felt (even if she didn't, it was the razzmatazz that mattered) and how vital it was for women to check their breasts regularly for any abnormality, something we had failed to do. She added that if they ever noticed anything untoward, they should not hesitate to go their doctor immediately.

The idea that we should limit ourselves to performing plays that made no physical demands upon her had been quickly forgotten. She used all her skills to put herself over as a lively, healthy woman who fully intended to live until she was a hundred.

However, she had been badly scared, and going out to the audience – sometimes going over the top to get the message home – helped her to overcome her fears. We were both anxious about the future. We stepped up the practice of rib reserve breathing exercises learnt all those years ago at Central School of Speech and Drama – and they worked. I knew immediately when Marianne was suffering from panic because her breathing became steadier and deeper than usual, and she would look extremely calm.

We had only lost twelve days out of a full season of playing every night, including Sundays. Feeling very pleased with herself on that count, she returned to the Infirmary for a routine check. We received a shock. She learnt that two tumours had been removed as one had been hiding behind the other. A few cancer cells had also been located in the lymph gland under the left armpit. It was now imperative for her to undergo radiotherapy; she was registered for a long session at the end of the summer season.

We had plenty to occupy ourselves – acting, writing letters, organising the next tour – which helped divert our attention from worrying too much about what we now knew. One afternoon, whilst we were icing the next batch of chocolate cakes, the stage manager walked into the kitchen and said there was someone waiting in the theatre foyer who wanted to speak to us.

We had long since given up anticipating what people might want when they asked to see us off-stage. It could be a manuscript for us to read, a 'Mrs Worthington' with a daughter longing to go on the stage, a friend of the family who'd come to say 'hello', a cook book or a picture to be sold, an American tourist waiting to photograph us. This time, however, it was Dr Colin Campbell, Senior Tutor of Churchill College, Cambridge, on holiday on Mull. His request was unusual – indeed, we were neither of us quite sure what it meant. He invited us to apply to his college for Fellow Commonerships. It was not often we found ourselves at a loss for something to say, but his talk of Churchill College and Fellow Commonerships perplexed us. All we could do was look brightly interested and repeat the phrase, 'Fellow Commonerships?' – as people do when they haven't understood.

Dr Campbell's answer didn't get us much further. 'Sort of actors in residence?' we ventured. 'Not quite,' he replied. He said little else, except to suggest, 'Wait until Marianne is over her radiotherapy, then send us your CVs.' We watched him leave with his wife, Margaret. They smiled at us as they went. 'What a laconic man!' said Marianne.

A little later, with the season behind us, Marianne and I were staying in Glasgow at a University hall of residence while she attended the Belvedere Hospital for radiotherapy – 'cooking', as she called it. A strange entry in my diary reflects something of the way I was reacting to the stresses imposed by the cancer and the long season, which had begun on such a note of hope with the Royal Garden Party, the wedding and the film. It seems that, during that particular week, I was definitely 'off' women. Their oddness, their moods, their periods and the menopause; their toughness and delicacy; their practicality and sound common sense that so often deflated masculine dreams; all this came under attack. Women were the target for all my pent-up anger, fear and frustration. I rounded off the entry, 'No wonder I feel I'll die before she does.' This was, of course, irrational. Nevertheless, it was a mark of my despair.

I was less grumpy a few days later when, on a fresh morning, with little white clouds scudding low across a pale blue sky, Marianne and I walked very slowly into Byres Road in Glasgow to buy her a patchwork skirt. This had a good effect on both of us.

On returning to our room, we found a *Daily Express* photographer who had come to take a picture of Marianne for an article that had been written about her. At the smell of publicity, despite her soporific condition, she perked up and gave of her best. After he had gone, she wept. The therapy was having a depressing effect, added to which she was fully aware that, no matter how good the treatment she was receiving, there was always a chance that she was, as she put it, 'booked'.

For the first time, we talked seriously about death. It was hard. She spent the next two weeks having treatment. For her, the worst part of the experience, beyond feeling so old and decrepit, was being left alone in the radiotherapy room. It was like a cell in a dungeon, she said.

Back home – and again surrounded by the people and things we loved – our spirits rose. The debilitating effects of the therapy began to fade. Work continued on all fronts, but Marianne was still too tired to contribute as much as she would have liked.

As ever, the cash flow remained a problem. To bring in money during the autumn – when we were engaged on management and rehearsal – I resolved to draw a Christmas card and print off a thousand of them on the duplicator. Within a month, we had managed to sell enough to bring in £200. This was not a princely sum but, again, it boosted our morale.

Marianne was regaining her health in a most encouraging way. The future was also beginning to brighten again. We drafted out an application to be elected as Fellow Commoners to Churchill College. Since meeting Colin Campbell, we had learnt that Churchill was a college with a bias towards the natural sciences and a very impressive academic track record. When she heard this, Marianne turned to me and said, 'What on earth do they want a couple of idiots like us for – as court fools perhaps?' Whatever reason, we looked forward to being accepted. We knew that living in college would be stimulating and very different from the kind of life we had been leading – a radical departure from our hair-raising brush with the Old Reaper.

The wound still pained her but, with a little ingenuity, we contrived to make love. That was a homecoming. Then, one evening, a very terrible thought occurred to me while we caressed each other. My fingers were tracing a pattern on her left breast. Suddenly, I grew bitterly angry. I saw that the demands of the theatre, the theatre that we ourselves had created, had curtailed the time for love. At the beginning of each season, we would withdraw from each other like surf ebbing from a beach; the time of love-making would not return until the theatre closed, usually in mid-September. We would look into each other's eyes and say, 'See you in the autumn.' Thus, there had been a period of four months during which the tumour could have grown undetected, and no opportunity for us to find the tell-tale lump.

16

'To walk the studious cloisters pale...'

The period set by the Infirmary for the routine checks on Marianne's health was every six months. It felt to me that she was playing Russian Roulette. As the appointment approached, an invisible gun was cocked and held in readiness to fire. With each X-ray, the trigger was pulled. As in the real game, the outcome was likely to be lethal. Marianne phoned me as soon as the result was through – the hammer had clicked home harmlessly. She had half a year's reprieve before the next round.

We now looked forward intensely to our sabbatical term at Churchill College. I wrote at the time:

> We're off that island, away from the theatre and all the associated worries! And here is London to catch up with: Woody Allen in *Manhattan*; San Marco horses stabled in the Royal Academy; and the ducks in St James's Park.

We swung along through the capital, feeling so free that Marianne dared to go about without her prosthesis. In the park, we noticed a young man studying the lopsided contours of her chest with great concentration. Marianne caught his eye and gave him a rueful smile; he coloured to the roots of his hair and hurried off. We ate ices, not minding the wasps; we were as happy as children let out of school.

We could not afford more than five days in London. Nonetheless we already felt revitalised and were quite ready to catch the train at Liverpool Street Station and set off for Cambridge.

Churchill College had been opened in the early 1960s. For the most part flat-roofed, it occupies a large area of ground a mile from the city centre. There is something about its design that reminds me of a science fiction command post. A grounded spaceship, camouflaged with an outer skin of dull red brick – its observation pods cleverly disguised as bay windows. However, the anorexic Stonehenge portal with its turnstile is a pale copy of a Gordon Craig stage set. It seems more in keeping with a National Theatre production of *Coriolanus* than with a residential college for young men and women (some of whom enter this building having just left their homes for the first time in their lives).

We were given keys to a well-equipped flat, one of several tucked away on the far side of spacious playing fields about two hundred yards from the main buildings.

We arrived a few days before the start of term. On the day the students came up, Cambridge was constipated with cars. Normally the city is swimming with bikes.

Hordes of frantic, hot, long-suffering parents drove up in front of the college and thankfully disgorged their young and hopefuls. We watched as they streamed in through the gates carrying suitcases, music centres, rubber plants, posters, fridges, extra chairs, bottles of brandy, 'cello cases and, in the arms of both sexes, a variety of soft toys.

Later, when we had settled in and were comfortably seated in the Senior Common Room, the Professor of Economics, Frank Hahn, came in brandishing *The Financial Times* intoning, 'I see nothing but doom and gloom; buy gold, buy gold.' This little phrase remained with us and was the seed from which Marianne and I developed *Ostrich*, our last major theatrical project together.

The students invited me to direct a play of my own choosing, one to which I have always been attracted, *The Insect Play* by the Brothers Capec. The rehearsals went well, though at first the students found the subject naive. This attitude soon underwent a radical change. Half-way towards the date of our first performance, the Soviet Union entered Afghanistan and the message the play contained was thrown into sharp relief against world events. From then on, things took on a new impetus.

As guests of the college, we were invited to meet the Master, Sir William Hawthorne, who had distinguished himself in the field of thermodynamics. A diary note:

He is tall and shy, but very willing to make contact. He has invited us to join him on one of his regular Sunday walks... At the appointed time, we went to the Master's Lodge and, together with a party of visiting scholars, we drove out to the Fens by car. In a straggling crocodile, we walked along the banks of a canal. Sir William displayed a mild eccentricity in his passion for inventing limericks about local place-names. We visited an old steam-driven pump engine; Sir William gave us a very clear description of how it had worked. On the return journey to the college, Marianne and I sat in the back of his car. Sir William was quiet and, believing him to be immersed in problems concerning the nature of heat exchange, we kept silent. Suddenly, he turned to us and asked, 'Can you think of a rhyme for 'There was a young lady from Fakenham?'

The term progressed and we got to know a number of students. For Marianne, this was a complete change and a welcome opportunity to rest. She had found walking very tiring and so stayed quietly in the flat reading and making friends. It wasn't long before she found herself in the role of agony aunt, especially to some of the female students. They had no one to turn to except, at the best of times avuncular, and at the worst, gruff and rather bullying male tutors. They told Marianne that they were likely to be offered comfort in phrases such as, 'You shouldn't be so sensitive' and 'Try to think like a man'.

During my stay in college, I decided to try out two experiments which I hoped would cast light on actor/audience relationships. Questions had begun to bubble up in my mind – for instance, about why I felt that audiences were quite different every night. Was it me or was it them? What were they up to when the lighting was too dim or too blinding for me to see them? Could I rely wholly on what my ears told me about them?

Could I do less to get the same effect? What might distract an audience from the main action of the play – that is, apart from someone desperately wanting to go to the loo or something similarly beyond my control?

When playing to an audience in a particular place, such as a mining town where the local industry creates dust, or in a farming region where there are allergies, how does the actor discriminate between pathological and bored coughing? I wondered why it was that when an awkward person was in the audience – that is, someone who emanates negative vibrations – more often than not they were to be found sitting on my, i.e. the actor's, far right? Was it coincidence, crowd dynamics, or merely a subjective observation?

The first experiment – a rather grand term for what I was attempting to do – was set up in the Cambridge University Audio-Visual Aids Department. I used two video cameras, one of which was focused on Marianne and myself, and the other on a small, invited audience. We presented a varied programme of prose, poetry and scenes from plays, while the cameras recorded everything we and the audience did. On playback, the two pictures, one from each camera, appear synchronised, one above the other, on the same screen. The result makes it easy to see, in great detail, how an actor's line or a single gesture can affect an audience and how responses and counter-responses can be developed between one individual and another until everyone, actors and audience alike, becomes involved.

What stays in my memory is how body language transmitted emotion across the audience rather like waves rippling across the surface of a pond. Depending on what kind of 'stone' we dropped into the pond, the response was almost always immediate; and there was one very quick-witted, sensitive student who signalled his reaction before anyone else. Without his involvement, I believe the audience would have been – not necessarily less responsive – but very different; in other words, the underlying rhythm of their response was unique to those particular group dynamics.

Whereas this project had developed out of a lifetime's work in the theatre, the other experiment sprang directly from being resident in college. Marianne and I had been using the college library to read up about early English theatre. I was reminding myself about how plays had been presented, not in formal theatres, but on carts, in inn yards and in the dining halls of the great houses.

Marianne pointed out that Churchill College, though modern, had adopted the traditional Oxbridge format for dining in hall. I thought how marvellous it would be to present a short play to the diners, in the pre-Shakespearean manner. The setting would make it as authentic to the period as could be managed today. The end of the Christmas term was in sight and, with only twenty-four hours to go, I imagined I had missed my chance. However, what I had not bargained for was the Cambridge spirit of daring-do. When I mentioned the idea to Tim Cribb, the Director of Studies in English, during the fag end of a bibulous party, he jumped at it and challenged me to go ahead in the little time there was left. Exhilarated by his enthusiasm, I soon found myself caught up in a whirlwind of activity.

The students, at least those who were sober enough to grasp the idea, were eager to get started; the rest were co-opted and did what they were told. Because time was pressing – all we had was twenty hours to cast, dress and rehearse a play that was not yet written – I suggested Margaret Thatcher's market economy as a theme, while the venue and target of our satire was to be Churchill College and its Fellowship. The plot was roughed out and the writing of scenes delegated. Because Marianne hoped to observe the effect of the play on an unsuspecting audience, everything was done in secrecy. With only minutes to spare, the cast, after spending a sleepless night and a long hard day rehearsing, was ready to go.

The Churchill dining hall is a large version of the great hall in a medieval manor. Whilst there is no dais to elevate hoi aristoi above hoi polloi, there is a long table that runs along the top at right angles to the other tables where students sit. The High Table is for the use of the Fellowship and their guests, presided over by the Master.

The hall was full that evening and, being both Christmas and the end of term, there was a buzz of excitement. The kitchen staff were at the ready, the Master rose to his feet, and the assembled company went quiet as he said grace in Latin.

Enter the Lord of Misrule in the shape of three women students, dressed in top-hats and the scantiest of black underwear. They burst in and began dancing round the High Table to a recording from *Cabaret* of Liza Minelli singing 'Money, money, money'. Each high-kicking lass targeted a bald-pated Fellow and planted a resounding kiss on the gleaming flesh.

Marianne and I had arranged to sit where we could observe both the Fellowship and students. That evening opened our eyes to what theatre must have been like in the days when performers directed all their attention to their benefactors, the lord and lady of the manor. In this case, as had been decided beforehand, the student-players addressed themselves almost entirely to the Master and Fellowship, just occasionally throwing a glance or a line towards their peers. The play, which was short and to the point, was a satire on college economics, in which the selling of first-class brains to Marks and Spencer was an important part of the story.

The students made fun of everybody they could think of and consequently everyone was on the lookout for a verbal dart flung or a dart which had struck home. Eyes that were tired from a hard term's study came to life – and how they flashed! It soon became clear that Power was the name of the game. The power of individuals and those who held office was being put to the test by these roguish players. For a brief time, they had arrogated to themselves the role of court fools, hell-bent on revelry and carnival.

Marianne had benefited so much from our stay in college that we extended it and were there for Christmas itself. We found ourselves taking part in another celebratory outing with Sir William:

We have been on a glorious, tipsy Christmas picnic with Sir William. A party of us, including foreign scholars, their wives and children, took off into the country where, with rugs, bottles of wine and loads of food, we encamped near an old ice-house. The Master himself had cooked two turkeys to a turn and the ladies had supplied quiches, sandwiches, and gateaux, to which Marianne added a batch of Mull Little Theatre chocolate cakes.

For a couple of hours, we enjoyed an idyllic, sylvan afternoon, bathed in sunlight and fanned by the lightest of winter winds. During the drive home, we talked to a visiting professor who had worked at Los Alamos on the original atomic bomb; he told us just how close we had been to a world conflagration at the time Marianne and I moved to Mull. A chilling thought.

17

Film, Cuts and Gongs

Whilst in Cambridge, we had continued with the theatre administration. This included making arrangements with the BBC for a film unit to visit us in the New Year. They were to make a half-hour documentary of our work for the *Arena* series. It was a thrilling prospect.

The film directors, Carol Bell and Rosemary Wilton, arrived very soon after we ourselves got back home. For two days, film making was held up because a wildcat strike at the BBC had stopped the *Arena* camera crew leaving London. However, a free-lance team was quickly recruited from the north of England. Although they were accustomed to covering big news items from Ireland and light entertainment from the northern clubs, they had little or no experience of shooting an arts documentary. The macho image they liked to project had the effect of putting the two women on their mettle and the tension generated between the two parties worked for the good of the finished product. The men were the necessary grit in the oyster; the result was a little pearl of a film. They recorded us at home and then, in snowy but sparkling weather, crossed with us to the mainland where they continued to do shots of us on our first date in Tayvallich.

The whole island benefited from having Carol Bell as one of our directors. She was so entranced by what she had seen of Mull that she brought it to the attention of a friend of hers, a fellow director who was looking for a suitable location for an epic thriller. He, too, liked what he saw and arranged to ferry his cast and crew over to the island to shoot *The Eye of the Needle*.

After finishing the 1980 tour, we made our traditional visit to London to catch up with a few shows. The first thing we did on arrival was to book tickets for a production of *As You Like It* at the National Theatre.

On the afternoon before the show, while Marianne rested in our bedroom at the Sloane Club, I went to Tottenham Court Road to buy a small piece of electronic equipment. We had arranged to meet in the foyer of the NT – which Marianne always alluded to as the Vatican – and would therefore be approaching the South Bank from opposite directions. At the height of the rush hour, I caught a train on the Northern line, Marianne on the District. Amongst the thousands of commuters getting on the tube at Embankment, I caught sight of a woman entering my compartment. 'What a fascinating face!' I thought, and then, rather as though I had been watching a photographic print develop, it dawned on me that it was Marianne I was looking at. She hadn't noticed me. I tapped her on the shoulder. 'Oh,' she said, turning round and smiling up at me with feigned simplicity, 'We were always destined to find each other.' A lady standing next to us went all starry-eyed at this real-life romantic encounter. I like to think she believed it was our very first meeting. This happy coincidence was followed by a production of such joy that we returned for a second helping the next night.

As ever on leaving the National, we walked across Hungerford Bridge. With each step, we were asking ourselves, 'How long?' At the back of my mind, I had a favourite quotation of Marianne's from Marlowe's *Doctor Faustus*, 'O lente, lente currite, noctis equi!' (O, horses of the night run slowly, slowly) a phrase that had now left the realms of poetic drama and invaded the real world. Over the years, like so many lovers, we had come to think of Hungerford Bridge as our very own. Now we had reached a point where there was no place for it in our future. Neither of us felt able or willing to speak about the sadness we felt. Never again would we stroll along together, stop, lean on the rail and watch the slow progress of the barges as the water passed under the bridge.

Our first grandchild, Gareth, was born on 12 July 1980. Marianne was thrilled; she bubbled over with enthusiasm about the new baby. She suggested to Nick that he might like to leave the mainland with his family and join us on Mull; quite apart from her delight about Gareth, there was a very pressing reason why she wanted to have Nick himself near us – and that was her failing strength. She could gesture on stage as eloquently as ever, but lifting and carrying, so much a part of our theatre life, was becoming a problem for her.

Nick and Fiona set up home in the hut that September. Marianne, Nick and I quickly got to work together to design a production of *Macbeth* which would involve a cast of puppets. Neither of us had any great liking for puppetry in general, but when the devil drives, needs must.[7] Between us, we devised a system whereby the dolls could walk, talk, move their faces and eyes, grasp lanterns, take hold of letters and wield swords. What is more, they were almost as large as we were – Macbeth himself was tall enough to look Marianne in the eye. To be left alone with them on a darkened stage was unnerving. We combined our various skills to make an exciting stereo recording of the play. This was a huge undertaking; the three of us supplied all the voices and each scene was backed by relevant sound effects. Like archetypal figures imbued with power or, indeed, the shadows of the Three Witches, we stood on stage in full view of the audience and manipulated the puppets which we held in front of us. However, in order to achieve the maximum suspension of disbelief in the onlooker, we dressed entirely in black, 'disappeared' and could soon be forgotten.

Although we had aimed the production at adults, our favourite comment came from a child of eight who, at the point when Macduff decapitated Macbeth most horribly, was heard to say, 'I wish Macbeth had won!'

It was at about this time that Marianne and I wrote our first full-length play together, a light comedy that drew on our experience of the Fellowship at Churchill College for copy. We called it *Ostrich*.

---

7 Puppets made an appearance in a number of our productions, including *The Tempest* (Caliban, Trinculo, Stephano and Ariel); *Macbeth* (the whole cast); *Willy Nilly*, a satire, written by Marianne and myself, on the subject of political correctness as seen through the eyes of Shakespeare; and *Waiting for the Train* by Iain Crichton Smith.

While *Ostrich* was being drafted, we had an invitation to take our production of Arbuzov's *Old World* to Germany. Up until then, our British tours, a staple part of our economy, had always frustrated our efforts to respond positively to the many requests we received to go on tour abroad. In 1981, the Bürgermeisterin of Hildesheim, Lore Auerbach, asked if we could get away from our duties for a fortnight in the autumn to visit and perform in her city.

That October, carrying our costumes for *Old World* in one suitcase, our personal belongings in another and – Heaven forfend – Lady Macbeth folded up in a haversack, we set off by public transport. The Lady accompanied us because we had been asked to demonstrate our puppetry at the University in Hildesheim and she happened to be the neatest, lightest and most versatile of the puppets. She was also the most mischievous. On our return from Germany, we heard that three members of the technical department at the theatre in Hildesheim had suffered minor accidents and been off work. We remembered how, at the very time the men had been incapacitated, Lady Macbeth had sat demurely beside us in our dressing-room, looking as though butter wouldn't melt in her mouth. Marianne suggested that she had refrained from putting a hex on *us* because we were responsible for getting her back to Scotland.

This mini-tour had been a great success and put new heart into us; so much so, that we could show that the parent Company was now well enough established to run without us. To this end, we decided to make arrangements to have our next summer season off the island and leave the Mull Little Theatre in the hands of two other performers.

In January 1982, six weeks before we set

Puppets and programme by Nick Hesketh for the 1982 production of Macbeth

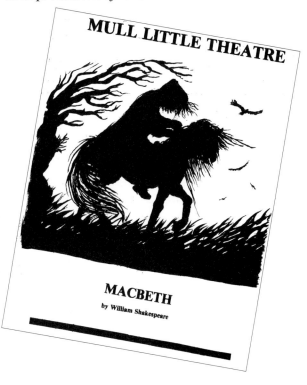

103

out on tour, Marianne was sitting on the hearthrug in front of the wood-burning stove. She was reading, with *The Scotsman* spread out in front of her. For a little while, I had been watching her trace a small circle on her lower lip with her little finger. She looked up and said, 'This is quite numb – feel.' She closed her eyes while, ever so delicately, I stroked the area. 'No, nothing,' she said.

We felt no great alarm because, up until then, cancer had meant pain.

So – no pain, no cancer. However, two months later, as we toured our pre-recorded *Macbeth*, she suddenly found herself in great distress. Her jaw ached abominably and she could hardly speak.

Since we happened to be within striking distance of the dental hospital in Bearsden, just north of Glasgow, we drove straight there. After various tests had been run, a consultant diagnosed teeth-grinding. It was not. A set of X-rays taken at the local hospital at the end of the tour showed it for what it was. Marianne had a secondary cancer in the jaw bone.

An investigation at the Royal Infirmary in Glasgow confirmed the presence of the cancer. The surgeon suspected that there were two sites, the other being situated in a rib. It was grim news. He then threw us completely off balance by saying that he would initiate treatment by removing her ovaries. This was such an unexpected development, so bizarre – comical even – that Marianne immediately felt more alert and better able to cope with what had overtaken her; her curiosity had been stimulated. The surgeon went on to explain the logic behind his decision. The cancer was feeding off her own oestrogen so, by removing those parts of her that were responsible for producing it, the tumour would starve. If all went well, it would regress; if the treatment was wholly successful, it would disappear.

By the time she went into surgery, her condition had deteriorated further; she could no longer open her mouth wide enough to receive a general anaesthetic. Instead, she was given an epidural and was therefore fully awake while the operation was being carried out. Knowing that she was intellectually curious as well as strong-minded, the surgeon asked her if she would like a mirror so that she could see how he removed her bits and pieces; but even Marianne's lion's heart faltered at that, and she declined the offer. Instead, the theatre team erected a little fence of green cloth, behind which they worked and kept her mind occupied with chat. I got a picture of her being in surgery with a team from *M.A.S.H.*

When I visited her shortly after her 'entertaining' operation – this was Marianne's own description – I found her in remarkably good spirits. She gave me hardly any time to catch up with her state of health before launching into a discussion of plans to take our plays to Ambleside in the heart of the English Lake District. My suggestion that we reschedule and wait until she was feeling fully recovered, was firmly dismissed as unnecessary. It was a great opportunity for us to show that we could expand just when things looked blackest. Marianne gave no house-room to doubts as to the satisfactory outcome of the operation; she was determined that she would be acting again in time for us to go ahead with the Lakeland venture.

When she got back from hospital, she wrote to our accountants:

... Herewith a sheet of figures – our takings since Easter... it's a pity my crisis made the Easter season pretty nominal. Had we been running at full tilt, I think we would have done really well... So, as you see, the theatre has done better this year than during the comparable period last spring.

It's a bit alarming being me at the moment, but I am very cheered to see that the figures on paper at least prove that the theatre here is so geared that we can cope with a crisis. When I look at the figures other theatres are turning in at the moment, I don't think we can be a major worry to the Scottish Arts Council...

Personally, I am taking it day by day. I am doing poetry programmes with fair ease. The three-part evening is a bit of a pull, to put it mildly. And the new play, *The Gin Game*[8], is proving very hard work – but possible...

B. and I go to Ambleside in about a month's time. Jackie Taylor and Brian James will carry on here. They won't do seven days a week, of course. We can't ask outside actors to do this... I hope very much the experiment will prove that this is a real working theatre which functions as such and is not dependent on the personalities of two crazy actors like B. and me. If the Ambleside thing works, we will plough back every penny in order for the company to afford to employ more actors to take our place next year... I can't be sure of a full, healthy life for the future – and touring as we have done up to now will hardly be practical. I shall have to have lots of hospital visits... I may enjoy a normal lifespan – they tell me to expect this, so I must expect it, too. But I am a cancer patient, and we need to be realistic! So thank goodness for good box-office returns! Love, Marianne.

She was still very weak when we took up residence at the Charlotte Mason College in Ambleside where we were to perform. However, she was convinced that the cancer was showing signs of regressing and, according to her, all she had to do was rest, act hard and put up with the artificially induced menopause (the result of the oophorec-tomy). Cold and hot flushes were coming fast and furious; she endured up to three a minute when exposed to the heat of the stage lighting. After each act, she would return to her dressing room with her costume wringing wet. During the performance, I could hear her blowing droplets of sweat off the tip of her nose.

On returning to the Highlands, we again went to the local hospital in Oban and, as Marianne had suspected, they confirmed that the cancer had disappeared; the damaged bone, all one and a half inches of it, had recalcified. This was the best news we had had yet. The result underlined the infirmary's confidence in her ability to fight a sustained battle against the disease. That day, we strode down the brae from the West Highland Hospital in Oban and looked with the greatest possible pleasure at the little shepherd's purse flowers that sprinkled the verge with dots of white – I don't think any flower could have looked lovelier.

The following November she wrote to her close friend, Dr Cathy Wright:

8 *The Gin Game* by D.L. Coburn.

Normandy Hotel
Renfrew
23 - 3 . 82

Barrie's sketch of Marianne on their last British tour together

Great news. On top of the fact that I get better all the time – I dropped all drugs and pain killers five days ago when I finished performing for this year, and my latest set of X-rays, blood tests and scans all came up nicely, thank you! – we have another smashing bit of news for the New Year. Again, we think it's a maybe/maybe not situation (will tell you as soon as we know!). I'll just tantalise you by saying it's not a family matter like a baby on the way or a marriage... To solve, look carefully in your newspaper on New Year's Day! If there's nothing about us, don't be surprised. I hope we are not going to be disappointed... we are probably just reserves, in case other people refuse and our names go in to take their places! Much love, M.

We were not reserves. In February 1983, kitted out in full fig, Marianne in a suit of navy blue and myself in top-hat and tails courtesy of Moss Bros, we took a taxi from a little hotel in Elizabeth Street and, feeling ridiculously important and excited, drove to Buckingham Palace. We were ushered up a wide flight of stairs into a large reception room full of pictures that I recognised, but only from reproductions. Here, we were graciously received by palace servants, officers, secretaries, footmen and a majordomo. We joined a large crowd of people milling about trying, like us, not to look as though they were the cats who had stolen the cream. A very grand person called us and gave explicit instructions as to how we should comport ourselves when it came to our turn to be presented to the Prince of Wales.

Rather alarmingly, Marianne and I were singled out and taken into an anteroom. We were an oddity. There was no precedent, as far as they were aware, for a husband and wife to receive their MBE medals together, and we had to practise going up to the dais as a couple. 'Walk forward as close as you can to the step so that the Prince won't be forced to lean over when he pins on your decorations. He sometimes comes perilously near to falling off.'

We joined a long queue in the ballroom where the investiture was taking place. In the background, a military band played selections from the Savoyards; they sounded slightly tipsy and this contributed to the jollity of the occasion. Friends and family of those who were receiving honours were seated in the body of the room, and the Prince – the Queen was abroad – stood stage centre. It was a like a grown-up version of a children's party at which we were all going to get a present.

'What a nice young man,' said Marianne, after it was all over. Talking to other recipients, we gathered that the Prince had something pertinent to say to everyone. To us, he said, 'Congratulations – I believe we have friends in common.' This was true, and of course it would hold good for *anyone* living on Mull; but it came as such a surprise and we were so flattered that it sent us into a flurry of who-do-we-know-who-he-knows kind of thinking. Neither of us could remember in detail what else he had said. I do recollect, however, that Marianne – always with publicity in mind – invited the Prince to the Mull Little Theatre and he said he would try. It was fun from beginning to end. As a piece of theatre, it was excellently stage-managed.

18

Progressions

For years, the sheep from the neighbouring farms had the run of our overgrown garden. In fact, there were times when they enjoyed the run of the house. This always occurred when the weather was miserably wet for both man and beast and the sheep found shelter next to our porch. Since burglary was virtually unknown on the island, we never locked up. Under normal circumstances, the catch on the front door was secure, but sometimes – at night, when we were fast asleep in bed – the weight of several sheep leaning against the door in an effort to avoid the worst of the rain, forced it open. Seeking warmth and protection, they would move warily and silently into the hallway.

The first I would know that we had been invaded was a tell-tale breeze blowing across my face, waking me up and bringing with it the unmistakable smell of wet wool. Knowing that I would have to close the door, I would slip reluctantly out of bed, struggle sleepily into my dressing gown and creep downstairs, hoping against hope that if the sheep had got in, my appearance would not frighten them; but it always did. As soon as they saw me, they went crazy. As I made a grab for the sheep nearest to me, one would invariably career into the living room while another headed for the office and the rest, hooves rapping out a hectic tattoo on the tiles, would disappear down the passage leading to the kitchen.

In the early days, I would be joined by Marianne and three delighted young boys, thrilled to have such an exciting excuse to get out of bed in the middle of the night. It was always a frightful business getting the animals back into the open air. As we grasped their horns, sending them into a frenzy of activity, they would butt us and crash against the wall, dragging us with them. Sometimes, in suicidal passion, they would hurl themselves to the ground where, as often as not, we would find ourselves slipping and sliding on our backs amongst them. The ewes, reacting to the bleating of their terrified lambs, would leap on and off chairs, in and out of the doorways and up the staircase into the bedrooms. Finally, having got rid of the woolly boarding-party, we were faced with cleaning up the mess. There would be the hallway awash with urine, green pellets squashed into the carpets and cushions, and muddy smears over the business letters which had been scattered all over the floor in the stampede. It was not a sight to gladden the heart at three o'clock in the morning.

In the early eighties, after a successful appeal to the Friends of the Little Theatre, we were able to put in a cattle grid at the gate to the grounds and mend the fences surrounding the property. The grid was installed primarily to protect both visitors and ourselves from the sheep, whose 'bahing' – so incessant, so loud, so badly timed – showed no respect for the performances. It was sad that the grid also kept out the cows. They had always been quite quiet and kept to their dragon paths. For the first time since we opened, Marianne and I missed hearing their gentle susurration as they passed by our dressing-room, pulling at the long grass.

Even so, no cattle grid could prevent the herding of sheep off the back hill. It wasn't our land and we had no control over it. Furthermore, there was only one sensible way for them to be brought off the heights and down on to the road; and that was along the path running close by the side-wall of the theatre. Imagine us, in the middle of a touching scene requiring our full concentration and all the sympathy an audience could muster, rudely interrupted by the thunder of small, sharp hooves urged on by the furious shouting of the shepherd. A thousand sheep (or what seemed like a thousand) had come to destroy the magic. They tumbled down the hill, crashing, bleating. We froze the action, held our dramatic pose and then, as the stampede rolled by, held again while a demoralised audience pulled itself together and revived from the effects of laughing themselves into fits. Held, that is, until we could go back to recreating the delicate bubble of emotion we had so carefully tended and nurtured during the previous thirty minutes.

The herding was inevitable. As each shearing time came round, we could only hope that Thespis would guide the shepherd towards a date in his calendar when his drive would coincide with the performance of a comedy and not a tender love story. The very last time it occurred (for us) was when we were well into a performance of *Ostrich*[9]. Marianne had reached a point in the play when she had to jam a waste-paper basket over my head. The audience were already laughing when the sheep descended upon us. The rumpus tipped the audience towards hysteria. Marianne, to her credit, topped it all by ad-libbing, 'And the professor of veterinary medicine ought to know better than to bring sheep into his office!'

During the interval when we performed *Ostrich*, the only way to reach the dressing-room from the stage – without meeting a member of the public – was through a trap door. This was done by crawling through the knee-hole of an old Victorian desk that dressed the set. On several occasions, Marianne got stuck. 'Give me a moment to unkink my back-bone,' she would say, and patiently wait for the pain to subside before delicately getting to her feet.

One evening, she misjudged her footing and fell over on stage. I moved across to help her but, managing to keep in character, she picked herself up and continued as if the trip had been part of the play. In the dressing-room she confided, 'I thought I'd had it. I thought, this is it, I'm going to die – but I didn't.' She went on to discuss how she should accommodate the character she was playing to the pain she felt. 'I'll play her a little older, I'll walk a little slower.' However, this restriction was a bitter blow – she always prided herself on her fine sense of space and timing. She could no longer dance through a part. Two days later, just before the half-hour call, she lost her balance again. This time, it was in the dressing-room. She cracked her head on a shelf. The skin round her eyes began to discolour at once and she felt very groggy. This accident only served to make her more than ever determined to go on. Applying Max Factor to the

9 *Ostrich*, (a comedy for two set in academia) by Barrie and Marianne Hesketh, published by Samuel French Ltd.

bruise, she said, 'I'm a soldier's daughter, Barrie!'

By not immediately asking for the doctor's opinion on this new turn of events, Marianne demonstrated that she wanted to take on the disease like a personal adversary and fight it on a different level than the purely medical. When she had first developed the secondary cancer, she said it was accompanied by a taste of naphtha (like mothballs); now, a week after her fall, the taste returned. She recognised it as a sign that the evil thing was on the advance. She could ignore it no longer.

Zoe, who had been our first front-of-house lady and who was a radiologist by profession, took an X-ray in the local cottage hospital. Then Marianne received a phone-call from her doctor with the news that there was a shadow on the spine; she remarked, 'Poor Zoe, that must have been a bad moment for her when she looked at the plate.' However, in saying that, she was putting up a very effective barrier. I found it almost impossible to enquire after her own response to the news. Like many military commanders facing battle, she was retreating into herself, summoning up her resources.

The great, black, Victorian Royal Infirmary opened its welcoming arms to her yet again. Instead of going to her old ward, she was sent hundreds of yards down subterranean passages to a brand new part of the hospital. The nurses were ready for her and greeted her like a member of the family. She had only one complaint about the new ward which was that the view from the windows was disappointing. From Ward 33 it had been, without doubt, lugubrious; but it was also visually very attractive – a fine panorama of Glasgow's Victorian necropolis.

Marianne's surgeon told us that the treatment he was now recommending would bring about another remission. This encouraged us immensely. He lifted our spirits further by telling us that the statistics were showing that women with a purpose have a greater chance of survival than those without. Marianne was certainly not without purpose.

She wrote to her friend in Sheffield:

Darling, don't worry! I am in little or no pain and the trouble, though tiresome, still has a good prognosis – truly. But I have a new patch of cancer – about the size of a ten cent piece – at the base of my spine... I've got a good chance of living 'till I'm ninety. They are going to give me six radio-cobalt treatments to zap it dead. Apparently, it is still the same kind of cancer – oestrogen-related – but a bit tougher! Everyone is being very kind: they are not hiding from me that the disease is dangerous... I'm going to have a little sleep now; radiotherapy makes one sleepy, I find! Marianne.

I was very alarmed at the way things were going and extremely concerned for her. When she knew what the treatment would be, she looked up at me from her hospital bed, drew me towards her and kissed me. 'Don't worry. They've got this thing taped. I'll be around to plague you all your life!'

Nick had had to take leave from the theatre for the time being, so we had engaged a young actor, Collin Johnson, a student from Central School of Speech and Drama.

When I accompanied Marianne to the hospital, he volunteered to hold the fort until I returned.

Entirely on his own, he saw people into the theatre and then, having made sure they were comfortably seated, he presented a one-man production of Shakespeare's *Henry V*. It was a tour de force.

Collin himself was a tower of strength. He helped make the interminable batches of chocolate cakes, developed an enchanting 'story-time' hour when Marianne was in hospital and later, at a moment's notice, when she was too exhausted from the treatment she was receiving, he joined me in presenting anthologies of prose and poetry.

His *Henry V* gave Marianne some of the happiest moments of her life in the theatre. Before performing it in the evenings, he always ran the lines during the afternoon. Occasionally, she would find the strength to cross over to the theatre, and there I would find the two of them: Collin rehearsing and Marianne listening with her whole being, absorbing the beloved words as if they, too, had something to contribute to her recovery.

On the day she left hospital, after her last dose of cobalt therapy, I took her through to Perth where all the family had gathered for a Highland wedding. Jim was marrying a nurse, Debbie, who worked at a local hospital. It was here in our hotel in Perth that we also met Karin, Richard's new wife, for the first time.

It was a wonderful occasion. The day was hot and cloudless. The bride and bridesmaids looked happy and flustered and Jim celebrated the day in formal Highland dress – velvet jacket, frilled shirt, kilt and sporran. The simple service was held in a little country kirk set in the midst of rolling pastures and fields of corn with a far vista of trees. After the ceremony, there was an exhausting ceilidh at which Marianne managed one, very dignified, fling. The rest of the time was given over to the consumption of astonishing quantities of liquor and wild Highland dancing. It was duly noted by some of the ladies, with amusement and approbation, that the gentlemen sporting the kilt were authentically dressed – or to be more accurate, undressed.

Notwithstanding her weak condition, Marianne was now looking forward keenly to the European tour that we had arranged to start almost immediately after the end of the summer season on Mull.

19

Travelling in Hope

Getting the balance right between maintaining a sense of purpose and hope in life, and accepting the alternative – that Marianne was likely to die sooner rather than later – was a taxing juggling trick and one I found difficult to handle.

In the light of what we feared, it was not practical to organise another tour for twelve months ahead; but in fact that is what we did. Like two hard-pressed rock climbers, we belayed our rope to sprigs of white heather and carried on climbing against the odds. Accordingly, we set our sights on the autumn of 1984 and wrote to theatres and universities in Germany, France, Denmark and the Netherlands. Marianne could help me do this during the day while she rested in bed. In the evening, she got up and joined me in the theatre, when it became business as usual.

Because writing *Ostrich* together had been so satisfying, she suggested I might think up another plot for us to work on. I drafted out a simple love story, in which the finding of an imaginary lost play by Bernard Shaw was an important element. It was actually while I was writing a few lines of mock-Shavian dialogue that we received a letter from Mrs Wheeler, a lady who lived in the north of England, offering us four hundred pages of unpublished letters between herself and Bernard Shaw. Her reason for contacting us was the hope that we might enjoy dramatising them. We were very struck by the coincidence. I was thrilled. Indeed, I was so excited that I dismissed out of hand Marianne's comment that transcribing the correspondence into play form might give me something to do after she had died. This was not something I wanted to acknowledge. It was an instance of how Marianne had got the balance right and I hadn't.

With Collin to help us, Marianne and I brought back into production the plays we had always felt safe with. Typically, because *The Bear* affirms life, she wanted to replay the explosive Madam Popova one more time. The cobalt treatment had done its work, her sense of balance had returned and though each performance totally exhausted her physically, the following day's rest built up a dam of energy on which she was able to draw. Towards the end of the play, there is a point when Smirnov, captivated by Popova, first grovels at her feet and then, springing to attention, clasps her close to him. The first evening we performed it this time round, I was so delighted to have Marianne back on stage that, for a moment, I forgot her fragile condition. I grovelled, kissed her foot, leapt upright, threw my arms around her and gave her a genuine hug of affection.

'Barrie!' she whispered fiercely in my ear, 'you'll break my back!' What she said was all too true. Before leaving hospital, she had been warned that her vertebrae were 'moth-eaten' and that even to attempt opening a heavy door might prove disastrous. I sprang away from her. From then on, the bear acted out his love for Popova at a distance – he dared not touch her.

We left Mull in the middle of September. Everything we needed for ourselves – *Village Wooing* (a salute to the opening of the Mull Little Theatre) and Marianne's version of *The Importance of Being Earnest* – was packed into two suitcases and a small haversack. Marianne had nothing to carry except her handbag.

We broke our European journey in Glasgow for an all-important check on her health. It was found that the cancer had now disseminated throughout her body; it was suspected that another 'hot spot' was developing on her spine. She was prescribed the new drug, Tamoxifen. Marianne wanted a prognosis, but nothing could be said for sure at this stage. We were left alone in an anteroom where we were given a quiet moment to adjust to the shock of what we had just been told. A nurse popped her head round the door to see if we were 'bearing up'. Rather tearfully, we assured her that we were. Like young lovers knowing that they must eventually part, we gazed steadfastly at each other, hoping to fathom in each other's eyes answers to questions as yet not quite formulated. Perhaps we were looking for intimations of immortality.

Three days later, we travelled by train through the Netherlands. We performed first in Arnhem and then in Amsterdam. Here, Marianne had promised herself a treat, a visit to the City Museum. However, her backbone gave her such trouble that she was unable to walk more than two hundred yards before we had to return to our hotel in the Damrak. As I helped her into bed, she apologised to me for being a nuisance.

By evening time, she felt much better and was determined to perform *The Importance of Being Earnest*. Her adaptation of this wonderful comedy retains all the characters. The intricacies of the play are preserved and so are the majority of the famous lines. Because it lasts no longer than half an hour, the action is fast and furious from beginning to end. She devised it in such a way that it was extremely clear and easy to understand. It proved to be the funniest production she ever did.

From Amsterdam we went on to De Bilt, where we were met by Professor Geo Dijkstra and his wife, Willy. They looked after us for several days during the week that we played Utrecht. Marianne was in pain and we thought the Tamoxifen was failing us. The Dijkstras' daughter, a doctor in the district of Groningen, arranged to see her when we performed there. Marianne kept up her morale by pointing out that the two signs which had always indicated an advance in the disease were now missing: she still liked coffee and there was no taste of naphtha.

We travelled from Groningen to Rotterdam and then to The Hague. We finished the Netherlands section of the tour at Eindhoven. Now, I felt, was a good time to make a decision. I looked at Marianne's pained face; she was relying heavily on make-up to hide the strain. Should we go on or go back? In answer to my query, she replied that she would stick it out a little longer.

When we got to Braunschweig, in what was then West Germany, we were made very welcome. By this time, Marianne had developed a terrible cold, but this made no difference. The tour was becoming a pilgrimage which she was determined to see through.

She had picked up an attitude of hostility to the Germans from her father, who had always seen them as the enemy after having fought against them through the First World

War and then been wounded on the Somme. In the Second World War he had been machine-gunned during a day-time attack on London, and showed his contempt and defiance in the only way he could. As the plane zoomed overhead, he picked up whatever was nearest to hand and hurled it with all the strength he could muster. It was a potato that he had grabbed out of the gutter.

Marianne herself had nearly lost her life when she was wounded on the head in the bombing raid that destroyed their home. However, our previous short visit to Lingen am Ems and Hildesheim had been sufficient for her to learn something about the people that was deeply significant to her. She now wanted to make her peace with them. From what she told me, it was as much for her father's sake as for her own.

We played ten small theatres within a forty kilometre radius of Brunswick. In the main, our German audiences proved to be a little less fluent in English than the ones in Holland; so, not wishing to lose our customers, we delivered our lines slightly slower. The tour continued to go well. Then, one afternoon, I nearly lost Marianne in a way that neither of us could have anticipated. An hour before the show at Wolfenbüttel, she was standing in front of a heavy wooden stage-set belonging to the host theatre. I jumped up on stage and the vibration weakened an insecurely fixed stage-brace. The large flat immediately behind her shook, teetered forward and fell down towards her.

Scene from Village Wooing, *on tour in Germany (Braunschweig), November 1983*

As it descended, the opening within it – where a door had yet to be fitted – slipped neatly over her. She remained where she was, shaken but alive. Had she been an inch further to one side or the other, her backbone would surely have shattered under the impact.

At Helmstedt, we had to shout to overcome the sound of torrential rain on the roof; it was like being at home. Then, not for the first time in her career, Marianne was surprised by a visitor as she was standing almost naked in the dressing -oom. After the show, she had stripped off down to her pants and was changing her bra when, unannounced, the local organiser walked in. As professional actors, we were very impressed by his 'quadruple take', a technique used in farce that requires a lot of skill if it is to appear natural. The first came when he caught sight of her; the second, when he quickly looked again to confirm what he thought he had seen – an all but naked lady; close on its heels came the third, a look of shock as he realised that she was missing a breast; and, finally, the fourth. This was held for a full two seconds as he stared, hypnotised by her Amazonian condition. By this time, Marianne had grabbed a jersey and was holding it in front of her.

This was just as well; the room was filling up fast with people eager to offer their congratulations. They had begun to force their way in and were all talking at once, excitedly and politely. But as they each took in the scene, the expression of good wishes got louder and the politeness more formal. It was some time before everyone was able to extricate themselves from what had now become an extremely embarrassing social situation.

Marianne had been pushing herself very hard. At three o'clock one morning, she sat up suddenly and pointed urgently towards the bathroom. I was only just in time to get a bowl for her. She was violently sick.

'Home!' I commanded. 'NO!' she shouted back. Over breakfast the next day, I asked her to stop, to think very seriously about returning. She replied, 'What is the point of living if I can't act!' She would not hear of the idea of going home, even though a lump was developing on her shoulder.

We travelled south to Stuttgart, where we gave two evening performances in a small theatre near the underground station. The following morning, Marianne woke feeling better than she had done for a long time; so, since we had a few days before starting out on the last leg of the tour, we decided to stay where we were and enjoy the parks and galleries.

Miraculously, she had no pain during what remained of that week. At the Castle Museum, we visited a little display of patchwork. Everything on show had been a dearly loved or greatly valued object that had suffered a break or a tear and then been mended. 'Perhaps,' she said, 'I should stay here as an exhibit.'

The pain returned soon after we set out for Bavaria. The diary covering this part of the tour is blank. I hadn't the heart to detail the daily deterioration – especially when set against the inspired performances Marianne was giving, night after night. Since leaving Stuttgart, the audiences had given us standing ovations and in so doing, they helped sustain her will to continue.

In Augsburg, the pain reasserted itself with a vengeance. She discovered that she could no longer sit down; the base of her spine could not support her weight. I grew exasperated with her. I tried everything to get her to go home: pleading, bullying, humouring – all to no avail. 'I've only three more shows to do. I'll see it through to the end.' On set, we dispensed with the chairs that were now redundant. She took pride in the fact that no one in the audience knew she was ill.

Finally, after twenty-three performances, we arrived at the ancient, attractive little town of Passau, set on a spit of land between two rivers. It was here, as we walked beside the romantic River Danube, that Marianne admitted a longing to be accepted back into the Roman Catholic Church but that her intellect would not allow it.

We found the theatre, built in the Scharfrichterhaus: its neat, whitewashed wall and small, well-kempt courtyard belied its bloody history. I now see it as a wry joke played upon Marianne by fate. She had first nurtured her dream of going on stage in the officers' quarters of an English prison; and it was to be here, in an old, public executioner's house in southern Germany, that she was to give her last performance.

The journey back was endured. As she got out of the train in Glasgow, she looked up at me, her face peaked with exhaustion and said, 'Daddy would have been proud of me.'

20

Taking Off

Marianne had her own personal picture gallery. As soon as she was comfortably settled in her hospital bed, she would set it up on the table beside her. First, there were the photographs of her family which she kept in a little wallet and always carried with her. Beside these, propped up against the books, were portraits of Garrick, Shakespeare and Hunter, the elegant, eighteenth-century, Glaswegian scientist. They were her 'regulars'. To these, she now added some reproductions of pictures by the German artist, Otto Dix.

As soon as she learnt that she was to be kept in for several days, she asked to see a Jesuit priest; there were points of faith that eluded her and she wanted to argue them through. I returned to the ward one afternoon, carrying bottles of fruit-juice and a little present of Anaïs-Anaïs perfume, to find her resting back on her pillows. Lying open on her lap was a book of Roman Catholic canonical law. She was abstracted and looked thoughtfully at me. 'Something funny; I've not been asleep but there were a lot of people on the other side of the glass partition. I thought I knew them. They were waiting for me – just waiting.'

On admission to hospital, she received treatment that enabled her to sit down in comfort. Her surgeon, assisted by a colleague, performed a small operation on the cancer seedling that had appeared on her shoulder during the tour of Germany. Since no theatre was available, she agreed to their suggestion that they do it without the usual paraphernalia. Previously, during a similar operation, Marianne had been surrounded by the full complement of theatre staff. The formal ritual had been observed: stretcher, table, green gowns, masks, scalpel, swab, etc. On this occasion, it could not have been more informal. To begin with, there wasn't a nurse in sight. After numbing the relevant part of her shoulder, the two surgeons set to work. Again, in my imagination, she was transported to the field dressing station in *M.A.S.H.* To keep her mind off the gore pouring down her front (Marianne had laughed at a joke and they had nicked a vein), the leading surgeon talked about his passion for fishing, especially about catching and cooking lobster. She wondered if we could dramatise the two different situations – it had so much comic potential, she thought.

She was put on a régime of chemotherapy. Almost immediately, she lost her hair. Because she didn't like the straggly bits that were left, she asked me to shave her head completely with a razor. I did so and left her in a thoughtful mood contemplating her reflection in a hand-mirror.

Jim had come over to the island to be with us for a few days. He walked into her bedroom and received the shock of his life. There was his mother, bald-headed, sitting up in bed, eyeing herself in her looking-glass and fingering sticks of stage make-up. I met him as he came downstairs in a state of considerable distress: he was worried that the disease had unbalanced her mind. We went back to the bedroom together to find Marianne, bright as a button, decorating her scalp with triangles, moons and stars in all the colours of the rainbow. She agreed that there was room for improvement but, as she had a well-shaped skull and loathed wearing wigs, she thought it was worth the experiment.

Back at home, and with the onset of spring, she could lie in our bedroom with the window open and watch the little birds pecking at a table Nick had constructed on the sill. Sometimes a chaffinch found its way into the bedroom and fluttered round her. This gave her great pleasure. Although she could only just walk as far as the bathroom – and that by leaning heavily on my arm – she was so bright that I told myself the worst was over, the doctor was wrong and all we had to do was have patience. The reality had become too bitter for me to face.

Seeing only what I wanted to see, I took advantage of this lift in her spirits and made a journey to Great Broughton near Cockermouth to visit Margaret Wheeler, the lady who had been in correspondence with Bernard Shaw. I was away for just three days. On my return through Glasgow, I bought Marianne a silk headscarf from Jaeger's. It had the colours that suited her best – blues and cobalt greens; but when I gave it to her, she picked at it as though unsure what it was. She laid it aside, and told me that she and Nick had had a long, comforting talk about what they thought happened to us after death. For me, this was a strange and very disquieting homecoming.

My hope for a future of acting together in the Little Theatre now faded altogether. The doctor had put Marianne on heavy doses of morphine. My sons and I talked to her but, most of the time, she was in a land miles away. She looked very happy. From time to time, she would wake and wave to us. Once, there was a sudden flash of recognition as she caught my eye; she winked at me and, for that moment, time dissolved and we were Barrie and Marianne together, as we had been in our youth.

She died in the early morning of 24 April 1984. Her family was at her bedside. I held her in my arms while she took off on the next stage of her adventure.

I said my final goodbye as she lay in her simple coffin, kissed her cold lips and slipped a copy of *A Midsummer Night's Dream*, her favourite play, beside her – a primitive, irrational action, but immensely comforting to me.

The funeral service was held in the house. Everyone on the island seemed to be there. They filled the room, crowded up the staircase and spilled out on to the drive. The day was full of sunshine.

The grave, dug close to the wall in the quiet and mysterious little patch of ground at Calgary, accepted the coffin. My tribute of three carnations thudded hollowly on the coffin lid… there was no one at home.

At my request, the stonemason carved an ancient Greek motif on the headstone: two faces, both laughing, one a satyr, the other a mask. She had been a bewildered Christian who saw that there was much to admire in paganism.

Carved at the foot of the stone are words from her favourite Shakespeare sonnet, 'Love alters not'.

Let me not to the marriage of true minds
Admit impediments. Love is not love
Which alters when it alternation finds,
Or bends with the remover to remove.
O, no! it is an ever-fixed mark,
That looks on tempests and is never shaken;
It is the star to every wan'dring bark,
Whose worth's unknown, although his height be taken.
Love's not Time's fool, though rosy lips and cheeks
Within his bending sickle's compass come;
Love alters not with his brief hours and weeks,
But bears it out even to the edge of doom.
If this be error, and upon me prov'd
I never writ, nor no man ever lov'd.

William Shakespeare, Sonnet 116

Index